MEDICARE AND SOCIAL SECURITY RETIREMENT GUIDE

Your Step-by-Step Manual to Avoiding Costly Mistakes, Maximizing Every Dollar You Deserve and Retiring with Confidence - Inspired by Sylvia A. Gordon's Professional Wisdom

DAVID HART

ISBN: 978-1-257-86590-1

Published by: Sharp Press

TABLE OF CONTENTS

INTRODUCTION

Picture this: You're turning 65 next month, and you thought you had everything figured out for retirement. You've been saving diligently, your mortgage is almost paid off, and you're looking forward to finally having time for all those hobbies you've put on hold. Then someone mentions "Medicare enrollment deadlines" and "Social Security claiming strategies," and suddenly you realize there's a whole maze of decisions ahead that could dramatically impact your financial security for the rest of your life. If this scenario sounds familiar, you're not alone—and more importantly, you've come to the right place.

Every year, millions of Americans approaching retirement face the same overwhelming challenge: navigating the complex web of Medicare and Social Security decisions that will shape their financial future. The stakes couldn't be higher. Medicare Part B premiums alone increased to $185 per month for 2025, up from $174.70 in 2024, and that's just the beginning. Make the wrong choice about when to enroll, which plan to select, or when to claim Social Security benefits, and you could be facing lifetime penalties, reduced benefits, or thousands of dollars in unnecessary costs. But here's the thing that keeps many retirees up at night: most of these costly mistakes are completely avoidable with the right knowledge and guidance.

Why This Guide Matters More Than Ever

This isn't just another generic retirement planning book gathering dust on your shelf. The retirement landscape has shifted dramatically, and 2025 brings significant changes that make this guidance more crucial than ever. Social Security benefits increased by 2.5% for 2025, with the average worker retirement benefit now $1,976 per month, up from $1,927 in 2024. While that sounds like good news, this 2.5% cost-of-living adjustment is actually the lowest increase beneficiaries have seen since 1.3% in 2021, highlighting the importance of maximizing every dollar you're entitled to receive.

Meanwhile, Medicare has introduced game-changing improvements that could save you thousands if you understand how to use them. Starting in 2025, Medicare Part D prescription drug plans now have a $2,000 annual cap on out-of-pocket costs, a significant improvement that could provide substantial relief for those managing chronic conditions or expensive medications. But like all Medicare benefits, you need to understand how this works and ensure you're positioned to take full advantage.

Perhaps most significantly, the Social Security Fairness Act was signed into law on January 5, 2025, eliminating the Windfall Elimination Provision (WEP) and Government Pension Offset (GPO). This change affects over 2.8 million people, particularly teachers, firefighters, police officers, and other public servants who previously saw their Social Security benefits reduced or eliminated. If you're among this group, you may be entitled to significantly higher benefits than you ever imagined possible.

The Hidden Costs of Confusion

Let's talk about what's really at stake here. Sarah, a recently retired teacher from Ohio, thought she was being smart by delaying her Medicare enrollment because she still had health insurance through her husband's employer. What she didn't realize was that his company had fewer than 20 employees, which meant Medicare should have been her primary insurance. When she finally enrolled 18 months later, she faced a lifetime penalty of 20% added to her Medicare Part B premium—that's an extra $37 per month for the rest of her life, totaling thousands of dollars she'll never get back.

Then there's Robert, who decided to claim Social Security at 62 because he was worried about the program's future solvency. He didn't understand that by claiming early, he permanently reduced his monthly benefit by about 25%. Over a 20-year retirement, that decision will cost him approximately $80,000 in lost benefits—money he worked his entire career to earn but will never receive because of one uninformed decision.

These aren't isolated cases. The number of people facing Medicare late enrollment penalties is growing. In 2016, only 60% of Medicare-eligible 65-year-olds were taking Social Security, compared to 92% in 2002. This shift means more people are navigating Medicare enrollment manually, without the safety net of automatic enrollment, and making costly mistakes in the process.

The Medicare and Social Security Learning Curve

Here's what makes Medicare and Social Security so challenging: they weren't designed to be user-friendly. These programs evolved over decades, with layers of rules, exceptions, and nuances that can trap even the most diligent planners. Medicare alone has Parts A, B, C, and D, with different enrollment periods, coverage gaps, and penalty structures. Add in Medicare Supplement plans (Medigap), Medicare Advantage options, and prescription drug considerations, and you're looking at hundreds of possible combinations.

Social Security brings its own complexity. When should you file? How do spousal benefits work? What about divorced spouse benefits or survivor benefits? How does working in retirement affect your benefits? For 2025, the earnings limit for workers under full retirement age increased to $23,400, with $1 deducted from benefits for each $2 earned over this limit. Miss this detail, and you could face unexpected benefit reductions.

The challenge is compounded by the fact that many of these decisions are permanent or extremely difficult to reverse. You can't go back and re-do your Social Security claiming strategy. Medicare late enrollment penalties last a lifetime. Choose the wrong Medicare Supplement plan, and you may never be able to switch to better coverage due to medical underwriting requirements.

What Makes This Guide Different

This guide draws from the professional wisdom of Medicare expert Sylvia A. Gordon, an attorney who has spent three decades helping people navigate these exact challenges. Her approach isn't theoretical—it's born from real-world experience helping thousands of retirees avoid costly mistakes and maximize their benefits. She's seen firsthand what works, what doesn't, and most importantly, what can go wrong when people try to figure this out on their own.

Unlike other retirement guides that give you generic advice, this book recognizes that your situation is unique. Whether you're still working at 65, planning to retire early, dealing with employer coverage that may or may not be "creditable," or trying to coordinate benefits with a spouse, you'll find specific strategies tailored to your circumstances.

We'll cut through the jargon and government-speak to give you clear, actionable guidance. You'll learn not just what to do, but when to do it and why it matters. More importantly, you'll understand how all the pieces fit together—how your Medicare choices affect your Social Security strategy, how your income impacts your Medicare premiums, and how timing can save or cost you thousands of dollars.

Your Personal Stakes in This Decision

Let's put this in perspective. The difference between making informed choices and stumbling through these decisions could easily amount to $50,000 or more over your retirement. Consider these scenarios:

Medicare Decisions: Choosing the right Medicare Supplement plan versus settling for an inadequate Medicare Advantage plan could save you $3,000-$5,000 per year in out-of-pocket costs. Over a 20-year retirement, that's $60,000-$100,000.

Social Security Timing: For a worker with average earnings, the difference between claiming at 62 versus full retirement age is about $500 per month. That's $6,000 per year, or $120,000 over 20 years.

Penalty Avoidance: Medicare Part B late enrollment penalties can add 10% to your premium for each year you delay enrollment. For someone who waits three years, that's a 30% penalty for life—adding over $650 per year to their Medicare costs.

IRMAA Planning: High-income Medicare beneficiaries can pay hundreds of dollars more per month in Medicare premiums based on their Modified Adjusted Gross Income. Smart tax planning and income timing can help you avoid these surcharges.

These aren't scare tactics—they're mathematical realities that affect real people every day. The good news is that with proper planning and understanding, you can avoid these pitfalls and potentially add tens of thousands of dollars to your retirement security.

What You'll Discover in This Guide

This comprehensive guide is organized to take you from Medicare and Social Security novice to confident decision-maker. We'll start with the fundamentals, ensuring you understand exactly how these programs work and what benefits you're entitled to receive. From there, we'll dive into the critical timing and enrollment strategies that can make or break your retirement financial plan.

You'll learn the insider secrets that most people never discover: how to coordinate Medicare with employer coverage, when delaying Social Security can add hundreds of thousands to your lifetime benefits, and how to structure your retirement income to minimize Medicare premium surcharges. We'll cover the nuances of working in retirement, the complexities of spousal and survivor benefits, and advanced strategies for protecting your assets from potential long-term care costs.

But this isn't just about avoiding mistakes—it's about optimizing your entire retirement health and income strategy. You'll discover how to use Health Savings Accounts as retirement tools, how to plan for the inevitable changes in your health and financial needs, and how to ensure your Medicare and Social Security choices support your overall retirement goals.

The Cost of Waiting

Here's something most people don't realize: the longer you wait to understand these programs, the fewer options you'll have. Medicare has strict deadlines—miss your Initial Enrollment Period, and you're stuck waiting for the General Enrollment Period, potentially facing penalties and gaps in coverage. Social Security benefits are calculated based on your lifetime earnings, but the claiming strategy you choose is largely permanent.

Every month you delay getting informed is a month closer to a deadline that could cost you thousands. The Medicare Annual Open Enrollment Period runs from October 15 to December 7 each year. If you're not prepared with the right knowledge, you might make another year of suboptimal choices.

Your Journey Starts Here

The decisions you're facing about Medicare and Social Security are among the most important financial choices you'll make in retirement. They'll affect not just your monthly budget, but your peace of mind, your healthcare access, and your overall financial security for decades to come.

This guide will serve as your trusted companion through every step of the process. We'll help you understand not just the rules, but the reasoning behind them. You'll learn to think like the experts who design these programs, understanding the incentives and protections built into each option.

By the time you finish this guide, you'll have the confidence to make decisions that align with your unique circumstances and goals. You'll know how to avoid the costly mistakes that trap so many retirees, and more importantly, you'll understand how to maximize every benefit you've earned through decades of hard work.

The knowledge in these pages represents the distilled wisdom of decades of professional experience helping retirees navigate these exact challenges. It's the same insight that has saved clients thousands of dollars and prevented countless costly mistakes. Now it's available to help you secure the retirement you've worked so hard to achieve.

Your secure retirement isn't a matter of luck—it's the result of informed decisions made with proper guidance. Let's begin this journey together, one step at a time, building the knowledge and confidence you need to make the smartest possible choices for your future.

CHAPTER 1: MEDICARE BASICS - DEMYSTIFYING THE ALPHABET SOUP

When Janet first received her Medicare card in the mail three months before her 65th birthday, she stared at it like it was written in a foreign language. Parts A, B, C, and D? Initial Enrollment Periods? Premium surcharges based on income? "I thought retirement was supposed to be simple," she told her daughter over coffee. "I've been paying into Medicare my entire working life, but I have no idea what I'm actually getting for my money."

Janet's confusion is completely understandable and shared by millions of Americans approaching Medicare eligibility each year. The Medicare system, while incredibly valuable, can feel like an alphabet soup of confusing options, deadlines, and decisions. But here's what Janet—and you—need to understand: Medicare isn't just a single insurance program. It's actually a comprehensive healthcare system with multiple parts that work together to provide different types of coverage. Once you understand how each piece fits together, the decisions become much clearer, and you'll be able to navigate your options with confidence rather than confusion.

What is Medicare and Who Qualifies?

Medicare is the federal health insurance program that provides coverage for Americans aged 65 and older, as well as certain younger people with disabilities and those with End-Stage Renal Disease (permanent kidney failure). Created in 1965 as part of President Lyndon Johnson's Great Society programs, Medicare was designed to ensure that older Americans wouldn't face financial ruin due to medical expenses during their retirement years.

Think of Medicare as your healthcare safety net—a program you've been paying into throughout your working career through payroll taxes. Every time you saw that "Medicare tax" deduction on your paycheck, you were contributing to your future healthcare coverage. Most individuals pay the full FICA tax so the QCs they earn can be used to meet the requirements for both monthly Social Security benefits and premium-free Part A.

Age-Based Eligibility

The most common path to Medicare eligibility is reaching age 65. If you're a U.S. citizen or have been a lawful permanent resident for at least five continuous years, you become eligible for Medicare the month you turn 65. Interestingly, if your birthday falls on the first day of any month, your Medicare coverage actually begins on the first day of the preceding month. So if you were born on December 1st, your Medicare coverage would start on November 1st.

Disability-Based Eligibility

You don't have to wait until 65 if you've been receiving Social Security Disability Insurance (SSDI) benefits for 24 months. This 24-month waiting period begins from the date your disability benefits start, not from when you first became disabled. Disabled individuals are automatically enrolled in Medicare Part A and Part B after they have received disability benefits from Social Security for 24 months. Certain conditions, like ALS (Lou Gehrig's disease), qualify you for Medicare immediately without any waiting period.

End-Stage Renal Disease (ESRD)

If you have permanent kidney failure requiring regular dialysis or a kidney transplant, you can qualify for Medicare at any age. Individuals are eligible for premium-free Part A if they receive regular dialysis treatments or a kidney transplant, have filed an application for Medicare, and meet one of the following conditions: Have worked the required amount of time under Social Security, the Railroad Retirement Board (RRB), or as a government employee.

Work History Requirements

To qualify for premium-free Medicare Part A (Hospital Insurance), you or your spouse must have worked and paid Medicare taxes for at least 10 years (40 quarters). You earn up to four work credits for each year you work. You'll qualify for premium-free Part A if you've earned at least 40 work credits during your lifetime. This means most people are eligible for premium-free Part A after 10 years of work.

If you haven't worked the required 10 years, you can still get Medicare, but you'll need to pay a monthly premium for Part A. In 2025, if you have 30 through 39 work credits, your Part A premium will be $285 per month. If you have fewer than 30 work credits, your Part A premium will be $518 per month.

Understanding Medicare Part A: Hospital Insurance

Medicare Part A is often called "hospital insurance," but that description doesn't fully capture everything it covers. Think of Part A as your coverage for "institutional care"—services you receive when you're admitted to a hospital, skilled nursing facility, or receiving certain types of home health care and hospice services.

What Part A Covers

Part A provides coverage for inpatient hospital stays, including your room, meals, nursing care, and most medications you receive during your stay. It also covers semi-private rooms, intensive care units, coronary care units, and specialized units like burn centers when medically necessary.

Skilled nursing facility care is another major Part A benefit, but it's not the same as long-term custodial care. You need to have received at least 3 days of inpatient hospital care in the last 30 days — this is called a qualifying hospital stay. Your stay in a skilled nursing facility must be ordered by a doctor who's enrolled in Medicare. You must require "skilled service," which is a healthcare service that only a professional, such as a registered nurse or physical therapist, can provide.

Part A also covers hospice care for terminally ill patients, as well as certain home health services when you're homebound and require skilled nursing care or physical therapy.

Part A Costs in 2025

Most people don't pay a monthly premium for Part A because they've earned enough work credits during their careers. However, Part A isn't "free"—you'll still pay significant out-of-pocket costs when you use these services.

The Medicare Part A inpatient hospital deductible that beneficiaries pay if admitted to the hospital will be $1,676 in 2025, an increase of $44 from $1,632 in 2024. The Part A inpatient hospital deductible covers beneficiaries' share of costs for the first 60 days of Medicare-covered inpatient hospital care in a benefit period.

Here's how Part A cost-sharing works for hospital stays in 2025:

- **Days 1-60:** You pay the $1,676 deductible, then Medicare covers the rest
- **Days 61-90:** You pay $419 per day
- **Days 91-150:** You pay $838 per day (these are called "lifetime reserve days" and you only get 60 of them total for your entire life)
- **Beyond 150 days:** You pay everything

For beneficiaries in skilled nursing facilities, the daily coinsurance for days 21 through 100 of extended care services in a benefit period will be $209.50 in 2025 ($204.00 in 2024). The first 20 days in a skilled nursing facility are covered at 100% by Medicare.

Understanding Benefit Periods

A crucial concept in Part A coverage is the "benefit period." A benefit period starts when you're admitted to a hospital or skilled nursing facility and ends when you've been out of both for 60 consecutive days. If you're readmitted after 60 days, a new benefit period begins, and you'll pay another Part A deductible. This means you could potentially pay multiple deductibles in a single year if you have separate hospital stays.

Medicare Part B: Medical Insurance Essentials

If Part A covers you when you're "in" somewhere (hospital, skilled nursing facility), then Part B covers you when you're "out and about." Medicare Part B is your medical insurance that covers doctor visits, outpatient services, preventive care, durable medical equipment, and many other healthcare services you receive outside of an inpatient setting.

What Part B Covers

Part B coverage is extensive and includes services most people think of as basic medical care. Doctor visits, whether in an office, clinic, or outpatient hospital setting, are covered under Part B. This includes visits to your primary care physician, specialists, and even second opinions when recommended by your doctor.

Preventive services are a major strength of Part B coverage. Annual wellness visits, most vaccines (including flu shots and COVID-19 vaccinations), mammograms, colonoscopies, bone density tests, and cardiovascular screenings are typically covered at 100% with no cost to you when received from participating providers.

Part B also covers outpatient surgery, emergency room visits (when you're not admitted), ambulance services, mental health care, and many diagnostic tests like X-rays, MRIs, and lab work. Durable medical equipment like wheelchairs, walkers, hospital beds, and oxygen equipment are also Part B benefits.

Medicare will pay for medically necessary physical therapy under Part B coverage. The services need to be ordered by your doctor to treat a condition or prevent a condition from getting worse — for example, physical therapy to reduce pain or to help you regain mobility after a stroke.

Part B Costs in 2025

Unlike Part A, virtually everyone pays a monthly premium for Part B coverage. The standard monthly premium for Medicare Part B enrollees will be $185.00 for 2025, an increase of $10.30 from $174.70 in 2024. This premium is typically deducted directly from your Social Security benefits if you're receiving them.

In addition to the monthly premium, Part B has an annual deductible. The annual deductible for all Medicare Part B beneficiaries will be $257 in 2025, an increase of $17 from the annual deductible of $240 in 2024.

After you meet your deductible, you'll typically pay 20% of the Medicare-approved amount for most services, while Medicare pays the remaining 80%. This 80/20 split is where Medicare can leave you with significant out-of-pocket costs, especially for expensive services or ongoing treatments.

Income-Related Monthly Adjustment Amount (IRMAA)

Higher-income Medicare beneficiaries pay more for Part B coverage through what's called IRMAA. If you file your taxes as "married, filing jointly" and your MAGI is greater than $212,000, you'll pay higher premiums for your Part B and Medicare prescription drug coverage. If you file your taxes using a different status, and your MAGI is greater than $106,000, you'll pay higher premiums.

The IRMAA surcharge can add hundreds of dollars to your monthly Medicare costs. For 2025, the surcharges range from an additional $74 per month for individuals with incomes between $106,000 and $133,000, up to an additional $444 per month for individuals with incomes of $500,000 or more.

Automatic Enrollment Considerations

Individuals already receiving Social Security or RRB benefits at least 4 months before being eligible for Medicare and residing in the United States (except residents of Puerto Rico) are automatically enrolled in both premium-free Part A and Part B. If you're automatically enrolled, you'll receive your Medicare card about three months before your 65th birthday.

However, if you're still working and have health insurance through an employer with 20 or more employees, you might want to delay Part B enrollment to avoid paying premiums for coverage you don't need. This is one of the most important decisions new Medicare beneficiaries face, and getting it wrong can result in lifetime penalties.

Medicare Part C: Medicare Advantage Plans Explained

Medicare Part C, better known as Medicare Advantage, represents a completely different approach to receiving your Medicare benefits. Instead of having separate policies for Part A, Part B, and potentially Part D, Medicare Advantage plans bundle everything together into a single plan offered by private insurance companies that contract with Medicare.

How Medicare Advantage Works

Think of Medicare Advantage as Medicare's version of an HMO or PPO plan. These plans are offered by Medicare-approved private companies that must follow rules set by Medicare and provide Medicare Part A (hospital insurance) and Part B (medical insurance) coverage, as well including drug coverage (Part D) in most cases, all under one plan.

When you enroll in a Medicare Advantage plan, Medicare pays the insurance company a set amount each month to provide your benefits. The insurance company then becomes responsible for covering all your Medicare-approved services, and they can do so with different cost structures, provider networks, and additional benefits than Original Medicare.

Medicare Advantage Benefits and Costs

The vast majority of Medicare Advantage plans for individual enrollment (88%) will include prescription drug coverage (MA-PDs), similar to 2024 (89%), and the share of MA-PDs that charge no premium (other than the Part B premium of $185 per month) is 67% in 2025, similar to 2024 (66%).

One of the most attractive features of Medicare Advantage plans is that they often include benefits not covered by Original Medicare. In 2025, 97% or more individual plans offer some vision, dental or hearing benefits, similar to 2024. These extra benefits can include routine dental care, vision exams and glasses, hearing aids, wellness programs, gym memberships, and even transportation to medical appointments.

In 2025, the average Medicare Advantage/Part C premiums are projected to range between $0 and $240+, with the estimated average plan this year costing $17 per month. Many Medicare Advantage plans charge no additional premium beyond your Part B premium, making them appear very attractive from a cost standpoint.

Medicare Advantage Limitations

However, Medicare Advantage plans come with trade-offs. In most cases, you'll need to use health care providers who participate in the plan's network; however, some plans offer non-emergency coverage out-of-network, but typically at a higher cost.

The provider networks in Medicare Advantage plans are often more restrictive than Original Medicare, which allows you to see any doctor or hospital that accepts Medicare assignment. If you have established relationships with specific doctors or prefer a particular hospital, you'll need to verify they're in your chosen plan's network.

Changes in Medicare Advantage for 2025

The number of Medicare Advantage plans that will be available to the average person is expected to decrease by 7%. This may result in less additional benefits being offered, smaller networks within plans, and an increase in overall out-of-pocket costs. However, the number of plans available in 2025 is still in the top three largest since 2010.

Despite fewer plan options, Medicare Advantage remains popular because of the additional benefits and often lower out-of-pocket costs compared to Original Medicare plus a Medicare Supplement plan.

Medicare Part D: Prescription Drug Coverage

Medicare Part D represents one of the most significant expansions of Medicare benefits since the program's creation. Added in 2006, Part D provides prescription drug coverage that can be obtained either through a standalone prescription drug plan (PDP) alongside Original Medicare, or as part of a Medicare Advantage plan.

Major Changes in 2025

The year 2025 brings revolutionary changes to Medicare Part D that will dramatically improve the financial protection for people with high prescription drug costs. Starting in 2025, Part D plan sponsors will provide their enrollees with the option to participate in the Medicare Prescription Payment Plan, which allows them to pay out-of-pocket prescription drug costs in the form of monthly payments over the course of the plan year instead of all at once to the pharmacy.

Most significantly, Starting Jan. 1, 2025, millions of Americans who get their prescription drugs through Medicare could get a major financial break when a $2,000 out-of-pocket spending cap on medications goes into effect. This represents a massive improvement from the previous $8,000 out-of-pocket limit.

How the 2025 Part D Benefit Structure Works

The new Part D benefit structure has been simplified into three phases:

1. Deductible Phase: For 2025, under the standard benefit, Part D enrollees will pay a deductible of $590 (up from $545 in 2024).

2. Initial Coverage Phase: After meeting your deductible, you'll pay 25% of your drug costs until your out-of-pocket spending reaches $2,000.

3. Catastrophic Coverage: Beginning January 1, 2025, people with Part D plans through traditional Medicare and Medicare Advantage plans with prescription drug coverage won't pay more than $2,000 over the calendar year in out-of-pocket costs for their prescription medications. Once you hit this limit, you pay nothing for covered drugs for the rest of the year.

Elimination of the Coverage Gap

The original Medicare Part D benefit had a coverage gap, also called the "donut hole," where enrollees were responsible for 100 percent of their prescription drug costs. This cost-sharing amount was eventually lowered to 25 percent. Even still, many enrollees who reached the coverage gap faced higher out-of-pocket costs while they were in that part of the benefit.

The good news is that this confusing and expensive coverage gap has been completely eliminated. As of Jan. 1, a person has the same cost-sharing from the time they meet their Part D plan deductible until they reach the new $2,000 out-of-pocket cap.

Part D Premiums and Plan Availability

The Part D late enrollment penalty is calculated by multiplying 1% times the "national base beneficiary premium" ($36.78 in 2025) times the number of full, uncovered months you were eligible to join Medicare drug coverage but didn't.

The average Medicare beneficiary has a choice of 48 Medicare plans with Part D drug coverage in 2025, including 14 Medicare stand-alone prescription drug plans (7 fewer than in 2024) and 34 Medicare Advantage drug plans (2 fewer than in 2024).

Special Protections for Insulin and Vaccines

Medicare Part D includes important protections for people with diabetes and those needing vaccines. Cost sharing will continue to be capped at $35 for covered insulins and $0 for Part D recommended adult vaccines. Since 2023, people with Medicare Part D coverage have paid no more than $35 for a month's supply of each covered insulin product.

Future Savings Through Drug Price Negotiations

In 2024, Medicare negotiated for the first time the prices of 10 of the most commonly used and expensive prescription drugs. The lower prices take effect in 2026 and are expected to save people enrolled in Medicare an estimated $1.5 billion in out-of-pocket costs in 2026 alone.

How Medicare Works with Other Insurance

Understanding how Medicare coordinates with other insurance coverage is crucial for making informed decisions about when to enroll and which coverage to maintain. Medicare's interaction with other insurance depends on several factors, including your employment status, the size of your employer, and the type of coverage you have.

Medicare as Primary vs. Secondary Insurance

When you turn 65, Medicare is generally considered to be your primary insurance, and any other coverage you have is secondary, unless you or your spouse has insurance through a current employer with 20 or more employees. This distinction is critical because it determines which insurance pays first and how much you might owe for medical services.

Employer Coverage Rules

If you're still working at age 65 and have health insurance through your employer (or your spouse's employer), the rules depend on the size of the company. For employers with 20 or more employees, your employer coverage typically remains primary, and you can safely delay Medicare Part B enrollment without penalty. However, if you work for an employer with fewer than 20 employees, you must sign up for Part A and usually need to sign up for Part B, which will become your primary insurance.

What Doesn't Count as Creditable Coverage

Other employer-related coverage, such as retiree coverage, COBRA coverage, or severance benefits, isn't considered to be primary coverage after you turn 65. That means if you don't sign up for Medicare, you may have gaps in coverage and be subject to a lifetime late-enrollment penalty.

Medicare and Health Savings Accounts (HSAs)

You can't contribute to a health savings account after you sign up for Medicare, but that doesn't necessarily mean that you have to stop making HSA contributions at age 65. If you or your spouse has health insurance through your current job, you can delay signing up for Part A and Part B and keep contributing to an HSA.

This is particularly important because HSA contributions can provide significant tax advantages, and HSA funds can be used tax-free to pay Medicare premiums and other qualified medical expenses in retirement.

Medicare and Medicaid Coordination

For people who qualify for both Medicare and Medicaid (often called "dual eligibles"), the programs work together to provide comprehensive coverage. Most people with Medicaid don't pay a premium for Part A. In most cases, your state will pay your monthly Part B premiums while you have Medicaid.

Dual eligibles also automatically qualify for Extra Help with Part D prescription drug costs, which can significantly reduce or eliminate prescription drug premiums and cost-sharing.

Marketplace Coverage and Medicare

If you have health insurance through the Healthcare.gov Marketplace (ACA plans), you need to make changes when you become Medicare-eligible. Your Marketplace plan may not renew your coverage at the end of the year. This means you and your family could have a gap in your coverage starting January 1 of next year. You won't qualify for help from the Marketplace to pay your Marketplace premiums or other costs.

Military Coverage (TRICARE) and Medicare

TRICARE and Medicare can work together, but the coordination rules are complex. Generally, if you have TRICARE and become eligible for Medicare, TRICARE becomes the secondary payer for services covered by both programs. You're not required to enroll in Medicare Part B if you have TRICARE, but doing so can provide additional benefits and reduce your out-of-pocket costs.

Veterans Affairs (VA) Benefits and Medicare

VA benefits and Medicare are separate programs that don't coordinate benefits. You can have both, and in fact, having Medicare might expand your healthcare options by allowing you to receive care from non-VA providers. However, the VA cannot pay Medicare premiums, deductibles, or other Medicare costs.

Understanding these coordination rules is essential for making smart decisions about when to enroll in Medicare and which other coverage to maintain. The key is ensuring you don't have gaps in coverage while also avoiding duplicate coverage that provides little additional value. The interaction between Medicare and other insurance can be complex, but with proper planning, you can optimize your coverage while minimizing your costs.

CHAPTER 2: SOCIAL SECURITY FUNDAMENTALS - YOUR FOUNDATION FOR RETIREMENT

When Tom celebrated his 40th birthday, his colleague mentioned something that stopped him cold: "You know, you're already halfway to earning enough Social Security credits for retirement." Tom had been watching "Social Security tax" come out of every paycheck but never understood what those deductions were building toward. Like most Americans, he knew Social Security would be "there" when he retired, but the mechanics remained a mystery.

Social Security is likely to be the foundation of your retirement income, providing inflation-protected benefits for life and potentially for your spouse after you're gone. For the average retiree, Social Security replaces about 40% of pre-retirement income. Understanding how the system works can help you maximize benefits and make strategic decisions that could add tens of thousands to your lifetime benefits.

How Social Security Works: Credits and Benefits

Social Security operates on a straightforward concept: you earn credits through work, and those credits qualify you for benefits. Think of it as insurance where your "premiums" are Social Security taxes and your "benefits" are monthly payments in retirement, plus disability and survivor protections.

Earning Credits

In 2025, you earn 1 Social Security credit for every $1,810 in covered earnings, with a maximum of 4 credits per year. You must earn $7,240 to get all 4 credits for 2025. You need 40 credits (10 years of work) to qualify for retirement benefits.

Extra credits beyond 40 don't increase your benefit amount. Your benefit is determined by the average of your earnings over your working years, not the total number of credits. The Social Security tax limit in 2025 is $176,100, meaning earnings above this amount aren't subject to Social Security tax and don't count toward future benefits.

Types of Benefits

Social Security provides three main benefit types:

- Retirement benefits: Monthly payments starting as early as age 62
- Disability benefits: Income if you become unable to work
- Survivor benefits: Income for your family if you die

The same work credits that qualify you for retirement also qualify family members for benefits based on your record. Spouses can receive up to 50% of your full retirement benefit, and children may qualify if they're under 18, disabled, or in high school.

Special Family Rules

For survivor benefits, credit requirements depend on your age at death—younger workers need fewer credits, with a maximum of 40. Under special rules, your spouse and children can receive benefits with just 6 credits earned in the 3 years before death.

Understanding Your Full Retirement Age (FRA)

Your Full Retirement Age (FRA) determines when you can receive full, unreduced Social Security benefits. Many assume it's 65, but that hasn't been true for decades.

FRA by Birth Year

Congress raised the retirement age in 1983 to account for longer life expectancies:

- Born 1943-1954: FRA is 66
- Born 1955-1959: FRA increases by 2 months each year (66 and 2 months to 66 and 10 months)
- Born 1960 and later: FRA is 67

The current full retirement age is 67 for people turning 62 in 2025. People born in 1959 will reach their FRA of 66 and 10 months throughout 2025.

Why FRA Matters

FRA serves as the benchmark for all benefit calculations:

- Claim before FRA: Benefits permanently reduced by 25-30%
- Claim at FRA: Receive full benefits
- Claim after FRA (up to age 70): Benefits permanently increased by 24-32%

FRA also affects the earnings test, spousal benefits, and survivor benefits. Understanding your specific FRA is crucial for optimal claiming strategies.

Calculating Your Primary Insurance Amount (PIA)

Your Primary Insurance Amount (PIA) is the monthly benefit you'd receive at Full Retirement Age. It's the foundation for all Social Security calculations.

Step 1: Calculate AIME

Social Security calculates your Average Indexed Monthly Earnings (AIME) using these steps:

1. Adjust past earnings for wage inflation

2. Select your highest 35 years of indexed earnings

3. Divide the total by 420 months (35 years)

If you worked fewer than 35 years, zeros fill the missing years, which is why working at least 35 years is beneficial.

Step 2: Apply the PIA Formula

For those reaching age 62 in 2025, the PIA formula is:

- 90% of the first $1,226 of AIME
- 32% of AIME between $1,226 and $7,391
- 15% of AIME above $7,391

These "bend points" ($1,226 and $7,391) increase annually. The maximum PIA for 2025 is $4,018.

Example Calculation

If your AIME is $5,000:

- 90% of $1,226 = $1,103.40
- 32% of $3,774 ($5,000 - $1,226) = $1,207.68

- Total PIA = $2,311.00 (rounded down)

The progressive formula replaces a higher percentage of income for lower earners while providing meaningful benefits for higher earners.

The Impact of Early vs. Delayed Retirement

The age you claim Social Security creates permanent differences in monthly benefits. The gap between claiming at 62 versus 70 can mean 75-85% more in monthly payments.

Early Retirement Reductions

Claiming before FRA permanently reduces benefits:

- Reduction: 5/9 of 1% per month for first 36 months
- Additional reduction: 5/12 of 1% per month beyond 36 months

For someone with FRA 67 claiming at 62 (60 months early):

- First 36 months: 20% reduction
- Next 24 months: 10% reduction
- Total: 30% permanent reduction

Delayed Retirement Credits

Waiting past FRA increases benefits by 2/3 of 1% per month until age 70—that's 8% per year. Someone with FRA 67 waiting until 70 gains 24% (3 years × 8%).

The Dramatic Difference

Using a $2,000 PIA example:

- Claim at 62: $1,400/month
- Claim at FRA (67): $2,000/month
- Claim at 70: $2,480/month

Over 20 years, the difference between claiming at 62 versus 70 is approximately $260,000 in lifetime benefits.

The Earnings Test

If you work while receiving benefits before FRA, earnings may reduce payments:

- Under FRA all year (2025): $1 deducted for every $2 earned over $23,400
- Year you reach FRA: $1 deducted for every $3 earned over $62,160 (only until FRA month)
- At FRA and beyond: No earnings limit

Key Considerations

Claiming decisions should factor in:

- Health and family longevity
- Current financial needs
- Employment status and earnings
- Spousal/survivor benefit implications

For married couples, coordinating claims can optimize household benefits and maximize survivor protection.

Social Security Cost of Living Adjustments (COLA)

Social Security's COLA protects benefits from inflation—one of the program's most valuable features.

How COLA Works

COLA is calculated using the Consumer Price Index for Urban Wage Earners (CPI-W). Social Security compares the third quarter (July-September) average CPI-W with the same period from the previous year. If there's an increase, beneficiaries receive a matching percentage increase.

The 2025 COLA is 2.5%, the smallest since 2020. This increases the average retirement benefit from $1,927 to $1,976 monthly—about $49 more per month. Over the last decade, COLAs have averaged 2.6%.

When COLA Applies

COLA adjustments apply to your PIA even before you claim benefits. This means your potential Social Security benefit grows with inflation whether you've filed or not. COLAs also increase spousal and survivor benefits based on your record.

The Compounding Effect

A $2,000 monthly benefit receiving 2.5% annual COLAs would grow to approximately $3,280 after 20 years—maintaining purchasing power throughout retirement. This inflation protection makes Social Security uniquely valuable for long-term financial security.

COLA and Claiming Strategy

Since COLAs apply before claiming, delaying Social Security provides double benefits: delayed retirement credits plus inflation adjustments on both your PIA and those credits. This compounding can substantially increase eventual benefits.

Medicare Premium Impact

Medicare Part B premiums are often deducted from Social Security benefits. While COLA increases gross benefits, Medicare premium increases can offset some gains. The 2025 Part B premium increased to $185/month from $174.70 in 2024.

Planning Considerations

Social Security's inflation protection makes it more valuable than fixed payments from other sources. A $2,000 Social Security benefit provides more long-term security than a $2,000 fixed pension because it maintains purchasing power over time.

COLAs are automatic—no action required. Beneficiaries typically receive notices in December detailing their new benefit amounts for the following year.

Social Security's combination of lifetime benefits, survivor protection, and inflation adjustment makes it the ideal foundation for retirement income planning. Understanding these fundamentals helps you make informed decisions about when to claim and how to maximize your benefits within your overall retirement strategy.

CHAPTER 3: MEDICARE ENROLLMENT - GETTING IT RIGHT THE FIRST TIME

When Susan received a letter from Social Security about Medicare three months before her 65th birthday, she almost threw it away. "I have great insurance through my job," she thought. "Why do I need to worry about Medicare?" Six months later, after retiring and losing her employer coverage, Susan discovered her mistake. She had missed her Initial Enrollment Period and would now face both a coverage gap and lifetime penalties. What should have been a seamless transition to Medicare became a costly lesson in timing.

Medicare enrollment isn't a "set it and forget it" decision—it requires understanding specific time windows and making strategic choices. Miss the wrong deadline or misunderstand creditable coverage rules, and you could face penalties that follow you for life. The good news is that Medicare's enrollment system, while complex, follows predictable patterns. Master these timing rules, and you'll navigate Medicare enrollment confidently while avoiding the expensive mistakes that trap thousands of new beneficiaries each year.

Initial Enrollment Period: Your 7-Month Window

Your Initial Enrollment Period (IEP) is Medicare's most important enrollment window—your first and best chance to sign up for Medicare without penalties. This 7-month period provides a crucial opportunity to establish your Medicare coverage, but understanding how it works can mean the difference between seamless coverage and costly mistakes.

The 7-Month Timeline

Your IEP begins 3 months before the month you turn 65, includes your birthday month, and extends 3 months after. For example, if you turn 65 in June, your IEP runs from March 1 through September 30. However, there's an important exception: if your birthday falls on the first day of any month, your IEP is calculated as though you were born the month before. So if you turn 65 on June 1st, your IEP runs from February 1 through August 31.

Coverage Start Dates Matter

When your Medicare coverage begins depends on when during your IEP you enroll. To avoid gaps in coverage, timing is crucial:

- Enroll 3 months before your 65th birthday: Coverage starts the month you turn 65

- Enroll during your birthday month: Coverage starts the month after you enroll
- Enroll in the 3 months after: Coverage starts the month after you enroll

Most experts recommend enrolling during the 3-month period before your 65th birthday to ensure seamless coverage without gaps.

What You Can Enroll In

During your IEP, you can sign up for all parts of Medicare:

- Medicare Part A: Hospital insurance (automatic if receiving Social Security)
- Medicare Part B: Medical insurance
- Medicare Part C: Medicare Advantage plans (alternative to Original Medicare)
- Medicare Part D: Prescription drug coverage

You also have what's called an Initial Coverage Election Period (ICEP) for Medicare Advantage and Part D plans. This period begins 3 months before your 65th birthday and ends either the last day of your Part B initial enrollment period or the last day of the month before you're enrolled in Parts A and B, whichever is later.

Automatic Enrollment

If you're already receiving Social Security or Railroad Retirement benefits at least 4 months before turning 65, you'll be automatically enrolled in Medicare Parts A and B. You'll receive your Medicare card about 3 months before your 65th birthday. While you can decline Part B if you have other coverage, you cannot decline Part A unless you withdraw your Social Security application entirely and repay all benefits received.

When You Don't Get Automatic Enrollment

If you're not receiving Social Security benefits when you turn 65, you must actively sign up for Medicare. This commonly happens if you're still working and haven't claimed Social Security. Medicare won't automatically notify you about your eligibility, so mark your IEP dates on your calendar and take action.

Disability-Based Eligibility

For those eligible due to disability, the IEP works differently. It begins 3 months before your 25th month of disability benefits, includes the 25th month, and extends 3 months after. Disabled individuals are automatically enrolled in Medicare Parts A and B after receiving disability benefits for 24 months.

The Stakes of Missing Your IEP

Missing your IEP without qualifying for a Special Enrollment Period triggers several consequences:

- Part B late enrollment penalty: 10% per year for each full year you could have enrolled but didn't
- Part D late enrollment penalty: 1% of the national base beneficiary premium for each month without creditable coverage
- Coverage gaps: You may go months without Medicare coverage
- Limited enrollment options: You'll have to wait for the General Enrollment Period

General Enrollment Period: Second Chances and Penalties

The General Enrollment Period (GEP) serves as Medicare's "second chance" enrollment window for those who missed their Initial Enrollment Period. While it provides an opportunity to get Medicare coverage, it comes with significant drawbacks that make avoiding it preferable.

When and How GEP Works

The GEP runs from January 1 through March 31 each year. During this period, you can sign up for Medicare Parts A and B if you missed your Initial Enrollment Period and don't qualify for a Special Enrollment Period. Your coverage begins April 1st of the year you enroll—meaning you could wait up to 15 months for coverage to start.

Part B Late Enrollment Penalties

The most significant consequence of using GEP is the Part B late enrollment penalty. This permanent penalty adds 10% to your Part B premium for each full 12-month period you could have signed up but didn't. The penalty applies to the standard Part B premium ($185 in 2025) and lasts as long as you have Part B coverage.

Penalty Calculation Example

If you waited 2 full years to sign up for Part B:

- Base penalty: 20% (10% × 2 years)
- 2025 penalty amount: $37 (20% of $185)
- Total monthly premium: $222 ($185 + $37)
- Lifetime cost: This $37 monthly penalty continues for life

Part A Penalties for Premium Payers

Most people get premium-free Part A, but those who must pay premiums face penalties too. If you delay Part A enrollment, your premium increases by 10% for twice the number of years you didn't sign up. For example, if you delayed 2 years, you pay the 10% penalty for 4 years.

In 2025, the full Part A premium is $518 monthly, so a 10% penalty adds about $52 monthly for the penalty period.

Limited Options During GEP

GEP only allows enrollment in Original Medicare (Parts A and B). You cannot:

- Enroll in Medicare Advantage plans
- Sign up for Part D prescription drug plans
- Get Medicare Supplement insurance in most states (due to medical underwriting)

This means you'll need to wait until the following October to add Medicare Advantage or Part D coverage during the Annual Open Enrollment Period.

Why GEP Exists

Medicare created GEP to prevent adverse selection—people waiting until they get sick to enroll. The penalties encourage healthy people to enroll when first eligible, maintaining a balanced risk pool. However, this system can be harsh on those who genuinely misunderstood the rules or received poor advice.

Strategies for GEP Enrollees

If you must use GEP:

1. Enroll early in the period: Don't wait until March—the sooner you enroll, the sooner your coverage starts

2. Plan for Part D: You'll face separate Part D penalties, so prepare to enroll during the next Annual Open Enrollment Period

3. Consider Medicare Supplement alternatives: Since Medigap may require medical underwriting, explore other gap coverage options

Special Enrollment Periods: When Life Changes

Special Enrollment Periods (SEPs) provide crucial flexibility for Medicare enrollment outside standard timeframes. These periods recognize that life doesn't always align with Medicare's rigid enrollment schedule, offering penalty-free enrollment opportunities when qualifying events occur.

Employment-Based SEP

The most important SEP involves current employment coverage. If you or your spouse work for an employer with 20 or more employees and have group health coverage, you can delay Medicare Part B enrollment without penalty. This SEP provides:

- Enrollment flexibility: Sign up any time while covered by employer insurance and still working
- 8-month window: After employment ends or coverage stops (whichever comes first), you have 8 months to enroll
- No penalties: Late enrollment penalties don't apply if you enroll during this SEP

Important Coverage Distinctions

Not all employer-related coverage qualifies for SEP protection:

- COBRA coverage: Not considered current employment coverage—won't protect against penalties
- Retiree health plans: Also don't qualify for SEP protection
- Small employer coverage: Employers with fewer than 20 employees may not provide adequate SEP protection

Moving SEPs

Permanent moves can trigger various SEPs:

- Moving outside your plan's service area: 2-month enrollment period
- Moving to an area with different plan options: May allow plan changes
- Returning to the U.S. from abroad: Special enrollment rights
- Moving into or out of an institution: Triggers enrollment opportunities

Loss of Coverage SEPs

Losing qualifying coverage creates enrollment opportunities:

- Loss of employer coverage: 2-month window after coverage ends
- Loss of Medicaid: Special enrollment rights for Medicare plans
- Loss of creditable drug coverage: 2-month window for Part D enrollment

Exceptional Circumstances SEPs

Starting in 2023, Medicare created new SEPs for exceptional circumstances:

- Natural disasters or emergencies: 2-month enrollment period
- Release from incarceration: Special enrollment opportunities
- Loss of Medicaid due to administrative issues: Protected enrollment rights

Plan-Related SEPs

Insurance company actions can trigger SEPs:

- Plan contract termination: Enrollment period to find new coverage
- Medicare sanctions against your plan: Right to switch plans
- Plan non-renewal: December 8 through February enrollment window
- Misleading information from plans: Corrective enrollment opportunities

2025 Changes for Low-Income Enrollees

Starting in 2025, new SEPs benefit low-income Medicare beneficiaries:

- Monthly SEP: Medicaid and Low-Income Subsidy recipients can drop Medicare Advantage monthly and return to Original Medicare
- Integrated D-SNP SEP: Enhanced enrollment opportunities for dual-eligible individuals in integrated Special Needs Plans

SEP Limitations and Rules

SEPs come with specific limitations:

- Limited timeframes: Most SEPs last only 1-2 months
- Specific qualifying events: You must meet exact criteria
- Documentation requirements: Proof of qualifying events may be needed
- One-time usage: Most SEPs can only be used once per qualifying event

How to Use SEPs

To utilize a SEP:

1. Identify your qualifying event: Ensure you meet SEP criteria

2. Act quickly: Don't delay—SEP windows are typically short

3. Gather documentation: Collect proof of your qualifying event

4. Contact Medicare or plan directly: Enroll through official channels

5. Confirm effective dates: Understand when your new coverage begins

Late Enrollment Penalties: What They Cost You

Medicare's late enrollment penalties are designed to encourage timely enrollment, but they can create significant long-term financial consequences for those who miss deadlines. Understanding exactly what these penalties cost helps illustrate why proper enrollment timing is crucial.

Part B Late Enrollment Penalty

The Part B penalty is Medicare's most common and expensive late enrollment penalty. It adds 10% to your Part B premium for each full 12-month period you could have enrolled but didn't. This penalty is permanent—lasting as long as you have Part B coverage.

2025 Part B Penalty Calculations

With the 2025 Part B premium at $185 monthly:

- 1 year late: 10% penalty = $18.50 monthly ($222 total)
- 2 years late: 20% penalty = $37 monthly ($222 total)
- 3 years late: 30% penalty = $55.50 monthly ($240.50 total)

Over 20 years, a 20% penalty costs an additional $8,880 in premiums. Combined with annual premium increases, the lifetime cost can exceed $15,000.

Part A Premium Penalties

Most people get premium-free Part A, but those who must pay premiums face penalties if they delay enrollment. The penalty adds 10% to the Part A premium for twice the number of years you delayed.

With 2025 Part A premiums at $285 or $518 monthly (depending on work history):

- 2-year delay: 10% penalty for 4 years
- Full premium penalty: $51.80 monthly for 4 years = $2,486 total penalty

Part D Late Enrollment Penalty

The Part D penalty is calculated differently but can also be substantial. It adds 1% of the national base beneficiary premium ($36.78 in 2025) for each month you went without creditable prescription drug coverage.

Part D Penalty Examples

- 6 months without coverage: 6% penalty = $2.20 monthly
- 12 months without coverage: 12% penalty = $4.40 monthly

- 24 months without coverage: 24% penalty = $8.80 monthly

The Part D penalty is permanent and continues even if you switch plans. Since the national base beneficiary premium can change annually, your penalty amount may fluctuate.

Penalty Calculation Timeline

Understanding when penalties start is crucial:

- Part B penalties: Begin from the end of your Initial Enrollment Period
- Part D penalties: Begin 63 days after losing creditable coverage
- Exclusions: Months with creditable coverage don't count toward penalties

Real-World Penalty Impact

Consider Maria, who missed her Initial Enrollment Period by 18 months:

- Part B penalty: 10% (one full year) = $18.50 monthly
- Part D penalty: 18% = $6.60 monthly
- Total monthly penalty: $25.10
- 20-year cost: Over $6,000 in additional premiums

Exceptions to Penalties

Some situations provide penalty protection:

- Special Enrollment Periods: No penalties if you qualify
- Creditable coverage: Employer or other qualifying coverage prevents penalties
- Low-Income Subsidy: Part D penalties don't apply to Extra Help recipients
- Exceptional circumstances: Natural disasters or other qualifying events

Penalty Appeals

If you believe a penalty was incorrectly applied:

- Request reconsideration: Use Medicare's formal appeal process

- Provide documentation: Submit proof of creditable coverage or qualifying events
- Equitable relief: Available in cases of misinformation or exceptional circumstances

Strategies to Minimize Penalty Risk

To avoid penalties:

1. Enroll during your Initial Enrollment Period: Unless you have qualifying current employment coverage

2. Maintain creditable coverage: Ensure any alternative coverage meets Medicare standards

3. Track coverage gaps: Never go more than 63 days without creditable prescription drug coverage

4. Understand employer coverage rules: Know when your employer coverage qualifies for penalty protection

Employer Coverage and Creditable Coverage Rules

Understanding how employer coverage interacts with Medicare is critical for avoiding penalties and ensuring seamless healthcare coverage. The rules are complex and depend on factors like employer size, employment status, and coverage type.

The 20-Employee Rule

The size of your employer significantly impacts Medicare enrollment decisions:

Large Employers (20+ employees):

- Employer insurance typically remains primary
- You can safely delay Medicare Part B without penalties
- Special Enrollment Period available when coverage ends

Small Employers (under 20 employees):

- Medicare becomes primary at age 65
- You should enroll in Medicare Part B to avoid gaps
- Employer coverage becomes secondary to Medicare

Current Employment Coverage

Only coverage based on "current employment" provides penalty protection. This includes:

- Group health plans from your current job
- Coverage through your spouse's current employment
- Plans based on your disabled family member's current work

What Doesn't Qualify

Several types of coverage don't provide penalty protection:

- COBRA coverage: Considered continuation coverage, not current employment
- Retiree health plans: Not based on current employment
- Severance benefits: Temporary coverage that doesn't qualify
- Individual marketplace plans: Don't provide creditable coverage for Medicare purposes

Creditable Prescription Drug Coverage

For Part D penalties, you need "creditable prescription drug coverage"—coverage that's actuarially equivalent to Medicare Part D. Common creditable coverage includes:

- Employer-sponsored prescription plans
- TRICARE prescription benefits
- VA prescription drug coverage
- Some state pharmaceutical assistance programs

Coverage Determination

Employers must notify employees whether their prescription drug coverage is creditable. You should receive:

- Annual creditable coverage notices
- Notices when coverage changes
- Confirmation letters when coverage ends

Keep these notices—you may need them to avoid Part D penalties.

Timing Your Medicare Enrollment

If you have large employer coverage:

1. Before age 65: Decide whether to delay Medicare Part B

2. At age 65: Enroll in Part A (it's usually free and doesn't interfere)

3. When employment ends: Enroll in Part B within 8 months using your Special Enrollment Period

If you have small employer coverage:

1. Before age 65: Plan to enroll in Medicare Part B at 65

2. At age 65: Enroll in both Parts A and B during your Initial Enrollment Period

3. After Medicare starts: Your employer plan becomes secondary coverage

Health Savings Account Considerations

If you have a Health Savings Account (HSA), Medicare enrollment affects your ability to contribute:

- HSA contributions must stop: You cannot contribute to an HSA once Medicare coverage begins
- Plan ahead: Stop HSA contributions 6 months before applying for Medicare (Part A has retroactive coverage)
- Use existing funds: HSA money can pay Medicare premiums and healthcare costs

Special Situations

Working past age 70: If you're still working with creditable coverage, you can delay Medicare without penalties, but there's no additional benefit since delayed retirement credits for Medicare don't exist.

Spouse's employment: If you're covered under your spouse's employer plan, the same rules apply—the 20-employee threshold determines whether you can safely delay Medicare.

Union coverage: Generally follows the same rules as employer coverage, but some union plans have special arrangements with Medicare.

Documentation and Record-Keeping

Maintain careful records of your coverage:

- Creditable coverage notices: Keep all notifications from employers
- Employment verification: Document your work status and employer size
- Coverage periods: Track exact dates of coverage to avoid gaps
- Plan details: Understand what your employer coverage includes

Common Mistakes to Avoid

1. Assuming all employer coverage is creditable: Verify your specific plan's status

2. Confusing COBRA with current employment coverage: COBRA doesn't provide penalty protection

3. Failing to track coverage gaps: Even short gaps can trigger Part D penalties

4. Not understanding employer size rules: Small employer coverage may not protect against Part B penalties

5. Ignoring spousal coverage implications: Your spouse's employment status affects your options

Making the Right Decision

Deciding whether to delay Medicare when you have employer coverage requires evaluating:

- Your employer's size and coverage quality
- The financial comparison between Medicare and employer premiums
- Your health status and provider preferences
- Your spouse's coverage situation
- Long-term employment plans

Understanding these employer coverage and creditable coverage rules is essential for making informed Medicare enrollment decisions that protect you from penalties while ensuring comprehensive healthcare coverage.

CHAPTER 4: SOCIAL SECURITY CLAIMING STRATEGIES - MAXIMIZING YOUR BENEFITS

When David turned 62, his neighbor congratulated him: "Now you can finally get your Social Security!" David had always assumed 62 was the "right" time to claim—after all, he'd earned it through 40 years of work. But three years later, after learning about claiming strategies, David realized his hasty decision had permanently cost him $400 per month for life. "I wish I'd understood that claiming early wasn't just getting my money sooner," he reflected. "It was accepting significantly less money forever."

David's experience illustrates a crucial truth: when you claim can be far more important than how much you've earned. The difference between optimal and suboptimal claiming strategies can easily amount to $100,000 or more over retirement. This chapter will equip you with the knowledge to make claiming decisions that maximize your lifetime benefits.

When to Start Taking Social Security Benefits

Your Social Security claiming decision revolves around three critical ages, each with permanent financial consequences:

• Age 62: 25-30% permanent reduction ($1,400 vs. $2,000 FRA benefit)

• Full Retirement Age (67): 100% of Primary Insurance Amount ($2,000)

• Age 70: Maximum benefit with delayed credits ($2,480 monthly)

Current data shows Social Security claims increasing in 2025, with higher earners unexpectedly claiming early at 62. This trend reflects baby boomer demographics and confusion about optimal strategies, but often represents costly mistakes that cannot be undone.

Early claiming makes sense if you have serious health concerns suggesting shorter life expectancy, immediate financial need without other income sources, or a high personal discount rate that values current over future income. Some spouse situations also favor early claiming to enable better household strategies.

Delayed claiming typically pays off when you have good health and longevity expectations, other income sources to bridge the gap, desire to maximize survivor benefits for your spouse, or lower current income that enables tax optimization. Bridge strategies involve using 401(k)s, IRAs, or taxable investments to fund early retirement years while delaying Social Security. This approach often maximizes lifetime benefits by allowing Social Security to grow at the guaranteed 8% annual rate while using other assets first.

The earnings test impacts those working while claiming before Full Retirement Age. In 2025:

• Under FRA all year: $1 withheld for every $2 earned over $23,400

• Year reaching FRA: $1 withheld for every $3 earned over $62,160

• At FRA and beyond: No earnings limit

The Break-Even Analysis: Early vs. Full vs. Delayed Retirement

Break-even analysis calculates how long you must live for delayed claiming to provide higher lifetime benefits than early claiming. Using a $2,000 FRA benefit example:

• Early (62) vs. FRA (67): Break-even at age 81

• FRA (67) vs. Delayed (70): Break-even at age 82.5

• Early (62) vs. Delayed (70): Break-even at age 80.4

Claiming early at 62 versus waiting until FRA creates an early advantage of $84,000 over the first five years, but results in a $600 monthly difference thereafter. The break-even point occurs at age 81, or 14 years after FRA.

Comparing FRA claiming at 67 versus delayed claiming at 70 shows the FRA advantage is $72,000 over the first three years, with a $480 monthly difference after age 70. The break-even point is age 82.5, or 12.5 years after age 70. The most dramatic comparison is early claiming at 62 versus delayed claiming at 70, where early claiming provides a $134,400 advantage over eight years but results in a $1,080 monthly difference thereafter.

Social Security data shows that a 65-year-old man has an average life expectancy of about 84, while a 65-year-old woman averages 86. For married couples, there's a 50% chance that at least one spouse will live to 92, which generally favors delayed claiming strategies.

Several factors complicate break-even analysis beyond simple life expectancy. Cost-of-living adjustments mean higher base benefits receive larger dollar increases over time. Tax implications can affect the net benefit difference, as higher benefits may increase your tax burden and Medicare premiums. Investment opportunities for early benefits and family benefit impacts also change the calculations.

Spousal Benefits and Claiming Strategies

Spousal benefits provide up to 50% of the higher-earning spouse's Full Retirement Age benefit, offering significant optimization opportunities for married couples. To qualify:

• Marriage to someone receiving Social Security

• Age 62 or older (any age if caring for qualifying child)

• At least one year of marriage

The maximum spousal benefit equals 50% of your spouse's Primary Insurance Amount and doesn't impact your spouse's benefit amount. However, spousal benefits are reduced if claimed before your Full Retirement Age and don't earn delayed retirement credits past FRA, unlike retirement benefits.

Starting in 2025, significant changes eliminated restricted application strategies for those reaching FRA after January 2, 1954. Social Security now automatically pays the higher of your own benefit or spousal benefit, simplifying the process but eliminating some optimization opportunities that previously allowed strategic timing between different benefit types.

Effective coordination strategies include having the lower earner claim early while the higher earner delays, providing immediate household income while maximizing long-term and survivor benefits. This approach works well for couples with significant earnings differences. File and suspend strategies remain available at FRA to earn delayed retirement credits, though suspending benefits also suspends family benefits, making timing coordination crucial.

The Social Security Fairness Act's repeal of the Windfall Elimination Provision and Government Pension Offset means government employees can now receive full spousal benefits that were previously reduced or eliminated, significantly improving retirement security for this group.

Divorced Spouse Benefits: What You Need to Know

Divorced spouse benefits provide crucial income based on an ex-spouse's earnings record, following specific rules that differ from spousal benefits. Eligibility requirements include:

• Marriage lasted at least 10 years

• Currently unmarried (lose benefits if remarry)

• Age 62 or older

• Ex-spouse eligible for Social Security (doesn't need to be claiming if divorced 2+ years)

Benefit calculations follow the same pattern as spousal benefits, with a maximum of 50% of your ex-spouse's Primary Insurance Amount, reduced if claimed before Full Retirement Age, and no delayed retirement credits past FRA. However, divorced spouse benefits offer several advantages: they're independent of your ex-spouse's claiming decision, don't impact your ex-spouse's benefits or their current spouse's benefits, allow multiple ex-spouses to each receive benefits, and include privacy protection since your ex-spouse isn't notified when you file.

Strategic considerations mirror those for spousal benefits. You should compare divorced spouse benefits with your own retirement benefit, as you can switch between them to optimize lifetime income. If you have multiple marriages lasting 10+ years, you can choose benefits based on whichever ex-spouse provides the highest amount. The same timing optimization principles apply, making break-even analysis valuable for decision-making.

The 2025 COLA increases the average divorced spouse benefit by about $23 monthly. When applying, you'll need your marriage certificate, divorce decree, ex-spouse's Social Security number if available, birth certificate, and proof of citizenship.

Survivor Benefits and Widow/Widower Strategies

Survivor benefits represent Social Security's most valuable benefit category, potentially providing 100% of the deceased spouse's benefit amount. Eligibility requirements include:

• Married at least 9 months (exceptions for accidental death)

• Age 60 or older (50 if disabled)

• Unmarried or remarried after age 60

Benefit amounts reach 100% of the deceased spouse's benefit at your survivor Full Retirement Age, which differs from retirement FRA. Those born in 1958 have survivor FRA of 66 and 4 months, those born in 1959 have 66 and 6 months, and those born in 1962 and later have survivor FRA of 67. Claiming at age 60 provides 71.5% of the full survivor benefit, increasing gradually until Full Retirement Age. Importantly, survivor benefits include any delayed retirement credits the deceased spouse had earned.

Unlike other Social Security benefits, survivors can use restricted applications to optimize lifetime income. One powerful strategy involves claiming a survivor benefit at 60 and switching to your own benefit at 70, providing immediate income when the survivor benefit exceeds your current retirement benefit while allowing your own benefit to grow with delayed retirement credits. This approach can provide $200,000 or more in additional lifetime income compared to standard claiming advice.

Alternatively, you might claim your own benefit early and switch to the survivor benefit at Full Retirement Age when the survivor benefit would be higher. This provides some income while preserving the full survivor benefit for later claiming.

Couples should plan strategically for survivor benefits by having the higher earner delay claiming to maximize the survivor benefit. Understanding that household income typically drops 33-50% when one spouse dies helps frame the importance of maximizing survivor benefits rather than just optimizing current household income. Both spouses should document strategies and account information to ensure smooth transitions during difficult times.

The application process requires applying by phone or in person rather than online. Applying promptly helps avoid lost benefits, though some retroactive payments are possible. Survivor benefits face the same taxation as retirement benefits and can qualify you for Medicare based on the deceased spouse's record, making them important for overall tax and healthcare planning.

CHAPTER 5: MEDICARE SUPPLEMENT VS. MEDICARE ADVANTAGE - THE GREAT DEBATE

You're standing at a crossroads, choosing between two fundamentally different Medicare paths. One offers freedom and predictability; the other provides convenience and potential savings. This choice affects your wallet, peace of mind, and healthcare access.

Medicare Supplement (Medigap) Plans A-N

Medigap insurance fills "gaps" in Original Medicare, covering deductibles and copays. These standardized plans (A through N) offer identical benefits regardless of insurer—you choose based on price and service.

Plan G is most popular for new Medicare beneficiaries, covering everything except the $257 Part B deductible. Plans K and L are cost-sharing options with lower premiums but higher out-of-pocket costs— K covers 50% of benefits until you reach $7,220 annually, L covers 75% until $3,610.

Most Medigap plans cover the $1,676 Part A hospital deductible, providing crucial protection against large unexpected costs. The beauty lies in predictability—after paying premiums and deductibles, additional costs are minimal.

Medicare Advantage: All-in-One Alternative

Medicare Advantage replaces Original Medicare through private insurers. In 2025, 76% of enrollees pay no premium beyond Part B's $185 monthly cost. These plans bundle Parts A, B, and usually D, often including dental, vision, and hearing benefits.

Average out-of-pocket limits are $5,320 for in-network services, with a maximum of $9,350 allowed. However, you're restricted to plan networks and may need referrals for specialists.

Comparing Costs, Coverage, and Networks

Traditional Medicare is accepted by 98% of physicians nationwide, while Medicare Advantage plans typically restrict you to network providers. Medicare Advantage averages $17 monthly premium but includes variable copays and deductibles.

Medigap offers predictable costs—higher premiums but minimal point-of-service expenses. Medicare Advantage provides lower upfront costs but variable expenses that accumulate toward annual limits.

International travelers benefit from Medigap plans C, D, G, M, and N, which cover 80% of emergency costs abroad.

When to Switch and When to Stay

Switching from Medicare Advantage to Original Medicare typically eliminates guaranteed-issue rights for Medigap, requiring medical underwriting unless you have special circumstances.

Consider leaving Medicare Advantage if providers leave your network, you need frequent specialist care, or face utilization management barriers. Recent analysis shows the top reason people switch from Advantage plans is difficulty accessing needed care.

Stay with Medicare Advantage if you're satisfied with network providers, appreciate integrated coverage, and benefit from supplemental services.

Regional Variations and Plan Availability

Four states—Connecticut, Maine, Massachusetts, and New York—offer guaranteed-issue protections for Medigap regardless of health status. Rural areas often have limited Medicare Advantage options, while urban areas provide more choices but potentially higher Medigap premiums.

In 2025, Medicare Advantage plan availability decreased 7%, though options remain substantial. Research local offerings carefully, as plan availability and provider networks vary significantly by county and region.

CHAPTER 6: PRESCRIPTION DRUG COVERAGE - PROTECTING YOURSELF FROM HIGH COSTS

Picture Maria, a 67-year-old retiree who takes medication for diabetes, high blood pressure, and arthritis. Without Medicare Part D coverage, her monthly prescription costs would exceed $800—more than many people's entire Social Security check. With proper Part D coverage, she pays less than $50 monthly for the same medications. This isn't just about saving money; it's about ensuring you can afford the medications that keep you healthy and independent.

Prescription drug costs represent one of the most significant and unpredictable expenses in retirement. Unlike other healthcare costs that might be occasional, medications are often daily necessities that you simply cannot skip. The good news is that 2025 brings revolutionary changes to Medicare Part D that dramatically improve protection against catastrophic drug costs. Understanding these changes—and how to navigate the Part D landscape—can literally save you thousands of dollars while ensuring you have access to life-saving medications.

Understanding Medicare Part D Plans

Medicare Part D operates on a fundamentally different model than traditional Medicare. While Parts A and B are government-run programs, Part D coverage comes through private insurance companies that contract with Medicare to provide standardized benefits. This public-private partnership creates both opportunities and complexities that every Medicare beneficiary needs to understand.

The Two Paths to Part D Coverage

You can obtain Part D coverage through two distinct routes. The first is through standalone Prescription Drug Plans (PDPs), which you add to Original Medicare alongside any Medigap coverage you might have. The second route is through Medicare Advantage plans that include prescription drug coverage (MA-PDs), which bundle Part D with your medical coverage in a single plan.

Each approach has advantages. Standalone PDPs offer maximum flexibility—you can choose the Part D plan that best covers your specific medications regardless of which company provides your medical coverage. Medicare Advantage plans with drug coverage provide simplicity and often cost savings through integrated benefits, but your drug coverage is tied to your choice of medical plan and provider network.

The Three-Phase Structure of Part D Coverage

Starting in 2025, Part D coverage consists of a three-phase benefit: a deductible phase, an initial coverage phase, and a catastrophic phase. This simplified structure represents a major improvement over previous years' more complex arrangements.

During the deductible phase, you pay 100% of your prescription costs until you meet your plan's deductible. No Medicare drug plan may have a deductible more than $590 in 2025, and some plans have no deductible. This means your maximum exposure during the deductible phase is $590, and many plans eliminate this phase entirely.

Once you complete the deductible phase, you enter the initial coverage period. In this phase, beneficiaries pay 25% of their prescription drug costs—typically in the form of coinsurance or copayments. This 25% cost-sharing continues until your out-of-pocket spending reaches $2,000 for the year.

When you reach $2,000 in out-of-pocket spending, you automatically enter the catastrophic coverage phase, where you pay nothing for covered medications for the remainder of the calendar year. This represents a dramatic improvement from previous years when beneficiaries could face thousands of dollars in additional costs even after reaching the catastrophic threshold.

Plan Selection Considerations

Choosing the right Part D plan requires analyzing several factors beyond just the monthly premium. The plan's formulary—the list of covered medications—is crucial. Each plan maintains its own formulary, organized into tiers with different cost-sharing levels. Generic drugs typically occupy the lowest-cost tiers, while specialty medications may require higher cost-sharing or prior authorization.

Network pharmacies also affect your costs and convenience. Most plans offer preferred pharmacy networks where your cost-sharing is lower than at standard network pharmacies. Some plans also offer mail-order options for maintenance medications, which can provide both cost savings and convenience.

The Medicare Plan Finder tool at Medicare.gov allows you to input your specific medications and compare total annual costs across available plans in your area. This analysis often reveals that the plan with the lowest premium isn't necessarily the most cost-effective option when you factor in your specific medication needs.

The Coverage Gap (Donut Hole) Explained

For years, the Medicare Part D "donut hole" represented one of the most confusing and financially devastating aspects of prescription drug coverage. Understanding what it was—and celebrating its elimination—helps illustrate just how significant the 2025 changes are for Medicare beneficiaries.

The Historical Context

The Medicare donut hole is another name for the Medicare Part D coverage gap. Prior to new Part D rules that took effect January 1, 2025, you would enter the donut hole when your total drug costs—including what you and your plan have paid reached a certain threshold. During this coverage gap phase, beneficiaries faced dramatically higher out-of-pocket costs, sometimes paying 100% of their medication costs until they reached the catastrophic coverage threshold.

The original Part D design included this gap as a cost-control mechanism, but it created perverse incentives and genuine hardship for people with high medication costs. Many beneficiaries found themselves rationing medications or skipping doses entirely when they entered the donut hole, leading to worse health outcomes and, ironically, higher overall healthcare costs.

The Gradual Closure and Final Elimination

The Affordable Care Act began gradually closing the donut hole, reducing the percentage that beneficiaries paid during the coverage gap phase. By 2020, the gap had "closed" in the sense that beneficiaries paid the same 25% cost-sharing in the coverage gap as they did during the initial coverage phase. However, the complex rules around what counted toward the out-of-pocket threshold remained, and many plans still had different cost structures during the gap phase.

As of 2025, the Medicare Part D coverage gap is eliminated. Instead, once your out-of-pocket prescription drug costs reach $2,000, you enter the catastrophic coverage phase—and pay nothing for covered medications for the rest of the year.

The $2,000 Revolution

The elimination of the donut hole and establishment of the $2,000 out-of-pocket cap represents the most significant improvement to Medicare prescription drug coverage since the program's inception. For Part D enrollees who take only brand-name drugs, annual out-of-pocket costs at the catastrophic threshold will fall from around $3,300 in 2024 to $2,000 in 2025.

This change is particularly beneficial for people taking expensive specialty medications. For the five drugs with the highest per capita Part D expenditures in 2021 used by more than 10,000 Part D enrollees – Revlimid, Pomalyst, Imbruvica, Jakafi, and Ibrance, all cancer treatments – annual out-of-pocket costs per drug in 2023 range from over $11,000 to nearly $15,000. Under the new system, regardless of how expensive your medications are, your annual out-of-pocket costs cannot exceed $2,000.

Practical Implications

The elimination of the donut hole simplifies medication planning and budgeting. Instead of trying to time expensive medications to avoid the coverage gap or rationing doses to stretch through the gap period, beneficiaries can now predict their maximum annual medication costs with certainty.

This predictability is particularly valuable for people managing chronic conditions that require expensive medications. Cancer patients, people with autoimmune diseases, and those requiring specialty biologics can now access their medications without fear of hitting an unaffordable coverage gap partway through the year.

Late Enrollment Penalties for Part D

The Part D late enrollment penalty represents one of Medicare's most misunderstood and financially punitive rules. Unlike most insurance penalties that you can eventually escape, the Part D penalty follows you for life once imposed, making it crucial to understand and avoid.

The Penalty Calculation

The Part D late enrollment penalty is calculated by multiplying 1% times the "national base beneficiary premium" ($36.78 in 2025) times the number of full, uncovered months you were eligible to join Medicare drug coverage but didn't. This formula means the penalty compounds based on how long you delay enrollment.

Example: If you waited 14 months after you were eligible for Medicare to join a Medicare drug plan, and you didn't have creditable drug coverage, you'll have to pay a 14% late enrollment penalty in addition to your monthly plan premium. Using the 2025 national base beneficiary premium, this would add $5.15 monthly to your Part D premium for life.

The Permanence Factor

The Part D late enrollment penalty is added to your premium for as long as you have Medicare drug coverage, even if you switch plans. This permanence distinguishes the Part D penalty from other Medicare penalties that might eventually be forgiven or reset. Once you've incurred a Part D penalty, it becomes a permanent addition to your monthly premium costs.

Creditable Coverage Protection

The key to avoiding penalties lies in maintaining "creditable coverage"—prescription drug coverage that's at least as good as standard Medicare Part D coverage. Creditable coverage includes:

- Employer or union prescription drug plans
- TRICARE prescription drug coverage
- Veterans' prescription drug coverage through the VA
- Medicaid prescription drug coverage
- Most state pharmaceutical assistance programs

If you have creditable coverage when you first become eligible for Medicare, you can delay Part D enrollment without penalty as long as you maintain that coverage. However, you have only 63 days after losing creditable coverage to enroll in Part D without facing penalties.

Special Enrollment Situations

Certain life events can trigger special enrollment periods that allow you to join Part D without penalties even outside the normal enrollment periods. These include:

- Moving outside your current plan's service area
- Losing employer or union coverage
- Gaining or losing Medicaid coverage
- Moving into or out of a long-term care facility

Understanding these special circumstances can help you avoid penalties even if you experience unexpected changes in your coverage situation.

Strategic Considerations

Even if you don't currently take prescription medications, enrolling in a basic Part D plan when you first become eligible can provide valuable insurance against future penalties. Many areas offer low-premium or zero-premium Part D plans that provide catastrophic protection while minimizing your monthly costs.

The Medicare Plan Finder can help you identify the lowest-cost Part D plan in your area. Even if you pay $20-30 monthly for a plan you don't currently use, this cost is far less than the lifetime financial impact of incurring a late enrollment penalty.

Extra Help and Low-Income Subsidies

The Extra Help program, formally known as the Low Income Subsidy (LIS), represents one of Medicare's most valuable but underutilized benefits. SSA estimates that Extra Help has an average annual value of $6,200, making it a significant source of financial relief for eligible beneficiaries.

Eligibility Requirements

Extra Help is available to people with income up to 150% of the Federal Poverty Guidelines/Levels (FPL). If your monthly income is up to $1,976 in 2025 ($2,664 for couples) and your assets are below specified limits, you may be eligible for Extra Help.

The asset limits vary based on your household size and marital status. Resources (such as savings, CDs, IRAs, stocks, bonds – not ones's home or car) can be no more than $17,600 (single) and $35,130 (married). Importantly, your primary residence and one vehicle are excluded from the asset calculation, focusing the test on liquid financial resources.

Automatic Qualification

Some Medicare beneficiaries automatically qualify for Extra Help without needing to apply. If you are enrolled in Medicaid, Supplemental Security Income (SSI), or a Medicare Savings Program (MSP), you'll be enrolled in LIS/Extra Help automatically. This automatic enrollment ensures that the most vulnerable beneficiaries receive benefits without navigating additional bureaucratic hurdles.

Benefit Levels

Extra Help comes in different benefit levels based on your income and assets. For those with the lowest incomes: With Extra Help, both the Part D deductible and plan premium are waived. In 2025, you will pay no more than $12.15 for each brand-name drug the plan covers ($4.90 for generic).

For those with slightly higher incomes but still within the Extra Help guidelines, benefits may include reduced premiums and lower cost-sharing, though not necessarily the complete elimination of all costs.

The $2,000 Cap Interaction

The interaction between Extra Help and the new $2,000 out-of-pocket cap creates even more powerful protection for low-income beneficiaries. Once your total out-of-pocket drug costs reach the catastrophic coverage threshold ($2,000 in 2025), you will have no copays. For Extra Help recipients, this threshold may be reached more quickly due to their higher medication costs relative to income, but their path to zero cost-sharing is now clearly defined.

Application Process and Timing

You can apply for Extra Help any time before or after you enroll in Part D. The application process involves providing detailed financial information to the Social Security Administration, which then determines your eligibility level.

Starting in 2025, if you have Medicaid or get Extra Help, you may be able to change your drug coverage once per month. This enhanced flexibility allows Extra Help recipients to adjust their coverage as their medication needs change throughout the year, rather than being locked into annual enrollment periods.

State Programs and Additional Assistance

Many states offer additional pharmaceutical assistance programs that work alongside federal Extra Help benefits. These State Pharmaceutical Assistance Programs (SPAPs) can provide additional premium assistance, coverage for medications not included in standard formularies, or help with cost-sharing that exceeds Extra Help limits.

Managing High-Cost Medications

The landscape for high-cost medications has fundamentally changed with the implementation of the $2,000 out-of-pocket cap, but smart strategies can still help you minimize costs and maximize access to needed treatments.

Understanding the New Cost Structure

For the five drugs with the highest per capita Part D expenditures in 2021—Revlimid, Pomalyst, Imbruvica, Jakafi, and Ibrance—annual out-of-pocket costs per drug in 2023 range from over $11,000 to nearly $15,000. Under the new system, regardless of how many expensive medications you take or how much they cost, your total annual out-of-pocket spending cannot exceed $2,000.

This cap transforms the financial planning around high-cost medications. Instead of potentially facing unlimited expenses that could drain retirement savings, you now have a predictable maximum annual exposure that you can budget for and plan around.

Manufacturer Assistance Programs

Even with the $2,000 cap, reaching that threshold represents a significant expense for many Medicare beneficiaries. Manufacturer assistance programs can help reduce your path to catastrophic coverage while providing access to medications that might not be on your plan's formulary.

Most major pharmaceutical companies offer patient assistance programs for their expensive medications. These programs may provide free medication for eligible patients, significant copay reductions, or coverage for medications during prior authorization appeals. The key is applying early in the year before you've exhausted other options.

Formulary Navigation and Exceptions

Each Part D plan maintains its own formulary with different tiers of coverage for various medications. Understanding your plan's formulary and exception processes can help you access needed medications while minimizing costs.

If your medication isn't covered by your plan or is placed in a high-cost tier, you can request a formulary exception. This process requires your doctor to demonstrate medical necessity and may involve trying alternative medications first. However, successful exceptions can significantly reduce your costs and help you reach the $2,000 threshold more quickly if you need multiple expensive medications.

Timing Strategies

The $2,000 cap resets each calendar year, creating opportunities for strategic timing of expensive treatments. If you're facing a choice between starting an expensive medication in November or waiting until January, the timing could affect whether you receive several months of free medication after reaching the cap.

For medications that can be safely timed—such as some preventive treatments or elective procedures—coordinating with your healthcare team to optimize the timing around the calendar year can maximize your benefits under the catastrophic coverage phase.

Pharmacy Network Optimization

Different pharmacies within your plan's network may offer different pricing for the same medications. Preferred network pharmacies often provide lower cost-sharing, while mail-order options may offer convenience and slight cost advantages for maintenance medications.

For expensive medications, even small percentage differences in cost-sharing can represent significant savings. A specialty pharmacy that charges 20% cost-sharing instead of 25% for a $10,000 monthly medication saves you $500 per month—money that also helps you reach the $2,000 threshold more quickly.

The Medicare Prescription Payment Plan

Starting in 2025, Medicare offers a new payment smoothing option for beneficiaries facing high medication costs. The Medicare Prescription Payment Plan starting in 2025 can help you manage your out-of-pocket costs for medications by billing you monthly capped amounts in lieu of paying upfront at the pharmacy. This program allows you to spread your annual out-of-pocket costs evenly across the year rather than paying large amounts early in the year before reaching catastrophic coverage.

Generic and Biosimilar Opportunities

Working with your healthcare team to identify generic or biosimilar alternatives can significantly reduce your medication costs while maintaining therapeutic effectiveness. Even with the $2,000 cap, using lower-cost alternatives when medically appropriate helps you reach catastrophic coverage more quickly and preserves financial resources for other healthcare needs.

The key is maintaining open communication with your healthcare providers about cost concerns while ensuring that any medication changes serve your clinical needs. Many physicians are willing to work with patients to find cost-effective alternatives when they understand the financial constraints involved.

Planning for the Future

The $2,000 cap provides unprecedented protection against high medication costs, but effective planning still requires understanding your medication needs, monitoring formulary changes during annual enrollment periods, and maintaining awareness of manufacturer programs and state assistance options.

By combining smart plan selection, strategic use of manufacturer programs, and effective timing of expensive treatments, you can minimize your path to catastrophic coverage while ensuring access to the medications that keep you healthy and independent throughout retirement.

CHAPTER 7: MEDICARE WHEN YOU'RE STILL WORKING PAST 65

The assumption that everyone automatically enrolls in Medicare at 65 is one of retirement planning's biggest myths. For Americans working past 65—whether by choice or necessity—Medicare enrollment becomes a complex decision intersecting with employer benefits, tax strategies, and long-term financial planning. Your choices during this transition affect immediate healthcare costs, coverage access, potential penalties, and retirement savings strategies for years.

Understanding Medicare while maintaining employment requires more than knowing when you can delay enrollment. You need to understand coordination of benefits, Health Savings Account impacts, creditable versus non-creditable coverage distinctions, and strategic timing for transitioning from employer coverage to Medicare.

Employer Coverage vs. Medicare: Making the Right Choice

Your decision between maintaining employer coverage and enrolling in Medicare at 65 depends primarily on your employer's size and your current coverage quality. These factors determine your eligibility to delay Medicare enrollment and which insurance pays first for medical care.

The 20-Employee Rule

Federal law establishes a clear dividing line at 20 employees that fundamentally changes your Medicare options. If you (or your spouse) are still working when you turn 65, Medicare works a little differently. If an employer has 20 or more employees, generally you can choose to delay Medicare enrollment, drop your employer coverage for Medicare, or have both Medicare and employer coverage.

For large employers (20+ employees), you have maximum flexibility. The employer cannot require Medicare enrollment and must continue offering the same health benefits available to younger employees. You can delay both Medicare Parts A and B without penalty, enroll in Medicare while keeping employer coverage, or drop employer coverage entirely for Medicare.

Companies with 19 or fewer employees can require you to enroll in Medicare Parts A and B when you turn 65 to continue receiving coverage through the employer. If you don't, you could end up with large coverage gaps.

Primary vs. Secondary Payer Status

Understanding which insurance pays first is crucial for financial planning and claims processing. For large employers (20+ employees), employer coverage serves as primary payer while Medicare becomes secondary. Your employer plan pays medical bills first up to coverage limits, and Medicare may help with remaining costs for services it covers.

With small employers (fewer than 20 employees), Medicare becomes primary payer even if you maintain employer coverage. Medicare settles your medical bills first, and the group plan pays only for services it covers but Medicare doesn't. This is why Medicare enrollment becomes essential for small-employer situations—without Medicare as primary coverage, you essentially have no meaningful health insurance.

The Part A Strategy

Even when working for large employers, many experts recommend enrolling in Medicare Part A at 65 while delaying Part B. Since most people qualify for premium-free Part A based on work history (40+ quarters of Medicare taxes), this coverage comes at no additional cost and can serve as valuable secondary insurance.

However, there's one significant exception: Health Savings Account eligibility. Medicare enrollees—including those who only enroll in Part A—are not allowed to contribute to an HSA, even if they continue to have coverage under an employer's HSA-qualified high-deductible health plan.

Special Enrollment Rights

If you delay Medicare enrollment while working, you're entitled to a Special Enrollment Period (SEP) providing an eight-month window to enroll without penalties. This process will let you sign up for Part A and/or Part B during the 8-month period that begins with the month after your group health plan coverage (or the employment) ends.

This protection eliminates Part B penalties as long as you enroll within eight months after losing qualifying employer coverage.

COBRA vs. Medicare: Understanding Your Options

COBRA continuation coverage and Medicare represent fundamentally different approaches to maintaining health insurance after leaving employment. Understanding their interaction prevents costly coverage gaps and unnecessary expenses.

The Mutual Exclusivity Principle

The most important rule: you generally cannot have both COBRA and Medicare simultaneously if you weren't already enrolled in Medicare when becoming eligible for COBRA. If you have COBRA before signing up for Medicare, your COBRA will probably end once you sign up.

This creates a crucial decision point: once Medicare-eligible, you typically must choose between continuing COBRA or enrolling in Medicare.

When COBRA Ends Upon Medicare Enrollment

For most people becoming Medicare-eligible while on COBRA, their COBRA coverage ends automatically when Medicare enrollment begins. However, if you were already enrolled in Medicare when becoming eligible for COBRA, you can maintain both forms of coverage with Medicare as primary and COBRA as secondary.

Cost Considerations

For most people, COBRA will be significantly more expensive than Medicare. This is because the average COBRA premium for an individual is around $600 a month, and much more expensive for a family. In contrast, Medicare Part B costs $185 monthly in 2025 for most beneficiaries, and Part A is premium-free for most people.

Coverage Scope Differences

COBRA provides identical coverage to what you had as an employee, including prescription drugs, dental, vision, and other employer plan benefits. Medicare focuses on core medical coverage through Parts A and B, with prescription drugs available through separate Part D plans.

Family Coverage Complications

An employee's entitlement to Medicare is a COBRA-qualifying event for the spouse and dependents only. Your family members may be eligible for up to 36 months of COBRA coverage even if you enroll in Medicare, which can be valuable if they aren't yet Medicare-eligible.

Health Savings Accounts (HSAs) and Medicare

The intersection of HSAs and Medicare creates one of retirement health planning's most complex areas. Understanding these rules is essential for anyone approaching Medicare eligibility who wants to maximize HSA benefits while avoiding tax penalties.

The Fundamental Incompatibility

Once you're enrolled in Medicare, you're no longer eligible to contribute to a health savings account. If you continue to contribute to an HSA after you have Medicare coverage, you could face tax penalties. This restriction applies to any part of Medicare—enrollment in Part A alone ends HSA contribution eligibility.

The Six-Month Lookback Rule

The most treacherous aspect involves Medicare's retroactive coverage rule. If you're signing up for Medicare after age 65, it's important to halt HSA contributions up to six months prior to your enrollment in Medicare. Medicare Part A coverage can be retroactive for up to six months when you enroll after age 65.

If you're eligible for premium-free Medicare Part A in May 2025 but don't enroll until November 2025, your Part A coverage would be retroactive to May 2025. Any HSA contributions between May and November would be considered excess contributions subject to penalties.

Strategic Planning for Continued Employment

Many people working past 65 face a difficult choice between continuing HSA contributions and enrolling in Medicare. If you work for an employer with 20+ employees and want to maximize HSA benefits, you might delay Medicare enrollment entirely.

If you choose to delay Medicare enrollment because you are still working and want to continue contributing to your HSA, you must also wait to collect Social Security retirement benefits. This is because most individuals collecting Social Security benefits when becoming Medicare-eligible are automatically enrolled in Medicare Part A.

Contribution Limits and Family Considerations

You may still contribute to your HSA even if your spouse enrolls in Medicare, as long as you remain an eligible individual for an HSA. For 2025, HSA contribution limits are $4,150 for individual coverage and $8,550 for family coverage, with an additional $1,000 catch-up contribution for those 55 and older.

Post-Medicare HSA Usage

While you cannot contribute to your HSA after enrolling in Medicare, you can continue using existing HSA funds for qualified medical expenses throughout retirement. You can use your HSA to pay Medicare premiums for Parts A, B, C, and D (though not for Medigap supplemental policies).

When Employer Coverage Isn't Creditable

"Creditable coverage" represents one of Medicare planning's most misunderstood aspects, yet has profound implications for prescription drug costs and potential penalties. With significant changes to Medicare Part D in 2025, many employer plans that previously provided creditable coverage may no longer meet the standard.

Understanding Creditable Coverage

Simply put, prescription drug coverage is creditable if it offers benefits at least as generous as Medicare Part D's prescription drug coverage. The importance cannot be overstated—individuals in non-creditable prescription drug coverage may face penalties for late enrollment in Medicare Part D.

The 2025 Creditable Coverage Crisis

The IRA significantly changed the Medicare Part D OOP annual costs cap from $8,000 in 2024 to $2,000 in 2025. As a result, many more employer-sponsored prescription drug plans might find it challenging to meet creditable coverage requirements and will be deemed non-creditable, especially Heath Savings Account (HSA) qualifying High-Deductible Health Plans (HDHPs).

High-Deductible Health Plans at Risk

HDHPs face particular challenges maintaining creditable coverage status under new rules. These plans typically have annual deductibles of several thousand dollars, and their out-of-pocket maximums often exceed $2,000 for prescription drugs alone. It seems unlikely that many HDHPs will be creditable after the 2025 Medicare Part D changes.

Notice Requirements and Timing

Employers must provide Notice of Creditable Coverage (NOCC) to all Medicare eligible individuals who are covered under, or who apply for, the entity's prescription drug plan (Part D eligible). This disclosure must be provided to Medicare eligible active working individuals and their dependents, Medicare eligible COBRA individuals and their dependents, Medicare eligible disabled individuals covered under the prescription drug plan and any retirees and their dependents at least once a year prior to October 15.

The Penalty Implications

Medicare Part D late enrollment penalties apply to individuals who go 63+ days without creditable prescription drug coverage after becoming eligible for Medicare. The penalty is calculated as 1% of the national base beneficiary premium ($36.78 in 2025) for each month of delayed enrollment, and this penalty remains for life.

Transitioning from Employer Coverage to Medicare

The transition from employer-sponsored health insurance to Medicare represents one of retirement planning's most complex healthcare decisions. This transition involves precise timing, coordination of multiple coverage types, and strategic decision-making affecting health coverage and costs for the remainder of retirement.

Timing Your Transition

The timing depends on several factors: when you stop working, when employer coverage ends, your age, and whether employer coverage is creditable. You have up to 8 months after you stop working (or lose your health insurance, if that happens first) to sign up for Part B without a penalty, whether or not you choose COBRA.

This eight-month window begins the month after you separate from your employer or the month after group health coverage ends, whichever happens sooner.

Coordinating Multiple Types of Coverage

During transition, you may temporarily have multiple types of health coverage. Understanding coordination helps ensure proper claims processing and cost management. If you enroll in Medicare while maintaining employer coverage, your employer plan remains primary while Medicare provides secondary coverage.

Once you leave employment, Medicare becomes primary coverage. This shift requires notifying healthcare providers about the change in primary insurance to ensure proper billing and avoid claim processing delays.

Strategic Enrollment Decisions

Your transition strategy should consider not just when to enroll in Medicare, but which parts to choose. Many people benefit from enrolling in Medicare Parts A and B while carefully evaluating options for prescription drug coverage (Part D) and supplemental coverage.

If your employer plan provided creditable prescription drug coverage, you can delay Part D enrollment without penalty. However, given changes to creditable coverage requirements in 2025, this strategy requires careful evaluation of your specific plan's status.

Medigap Timing Considerations

The transition creates important opportunities for Medigap coverage. You have guaranteed issue rights for Medigap policies for six months after enrolling in Medicare Part B at age 65 or older. However, timing is crucial—if you enrolled in Part B while working for a large employer and don't buy Medigap until after the six-month guaranteed issue period, insurers in most states can reject you or charge higher premiums based on health.

Financial Planning Considerations

The transition often involves significant changes in healthcare cost structure. Employer plans typically involve predictable monthly premiums with variable copayments and deductibles, while Medicare's cost structure depends on which parts and plans you choose.

Budget for Medicare Part B premiums ($185 monthly in 2025 for most people), potential Medigap premiums, and Part D costs. Medicare's cost-sharing structure may differ significantly from your employer plan, potentially affecting out-of-pocket costs for regular medical care.

Documentation and Record-Keeping

Maintain careful records of employer coverage dates, creditable coverage notices, and any gap periods between coverage types. These records are essential for proving eligibility for Special Enrollment Periods and avoiding penalties.

Keep employment records showing work dates, insurance certificates showing coverage periods, and creditable coverage notices from your employer. These documents may be required when applying for Medicare or later enrolling in Part D plans.

Provider Network Considerations

The transition to Medicare may require changes in healthcare providers if current doctors don't accept Medicare or aren't in your chosen Medicare plan's network. Traditional Medicare is accepted by 98 percent of all physicians and most hospitals in the U.S., but Medicare Advantage plans have more restrictive networks.

Research your providers' Medicare participation status before transition to avoid surprises. If you have ongoing relationships with specialists or need continuity of care for chronic conditions, this consideration may influence Medicare plan choices.

The successful transition from employer coverage to Medicare requires careful planning, precise timing, and strategic decision-making. By understanding rules governing Special Enrollment Periods, coordination of benefits, and various Medicare options available, you can navigate this transition smoothly while optimizing healthcare coverage and costs for retirement.

CHAPTER 8: SOCIAL SECURITY AND THE EARNINGS TEST

One of Social Security's most misunderstood aspects involves working while receiving benefits. Many people assume that claiming Social Security means permanent retirement from the workforce, but this couldn't be further from the truth. You can work and collect Social Security simultaneously, though certain rules apply that can temporarily reduce your benefits if you're under full retirement age.

Understanding the earnings test—how it works, what income counts, and when benefits are reduced—is crucial for anyone considering early Social Security claiming while maintaining some work income. These rules affect millions of Americans who need or want to continue working while drawing Social Security, whether to supplement their income, maintain health insurance, or simply stay engaged in productive work.

Working While Receiving Social Security Benefits

The fundamental rule is straightforward: when you begin receiving Social Security retirement benefits, you are considered retired for our purposes. You can get Social Security retirement or survivors benefits and work at the same time. However, there is a limit to how much you can earn and still receive full benefits.

The Basic Framework

The Social Security Administration doesn't prohibit working while collecting benefits, but it does impose earnings restrictions on people who haven't reached full retirement age (FRA). These restrictions only apply to earned income from employment or self-employment—they don't affect investment income, pensions, or other "unearned" income sources.

If you are younger than full retirement age and earn more than the yearly earnings limit, we may reduce your benefit amount. This reduction isn't permanent; it's more accurately described as a temporary withholding of benefits that you'll eventually recover when you reach full retirement age.

Full Retirement Age Considerations

Your full retirement age depends on your birth year. For people born in 1960 or later, full retirement age is 67. Starting with the month you reach full retirement age, there is no limit on how much you can earn and still receive your benefits. This means that once you hit your FRA, you can earn unlimited amounts without any impact on your Social Security payments.

The transition to unlimited earnings happens precisely at full retirement age, not at the beginning of the year you reach FRA. For example, if you reach full retirement age in August 2025, you can earn unlimited amounts starting in August, but earnings restrictions still apply through July.

Special Rules for Different Benefit Types

While most discussions focus on retirement benefits, similar earnings test rules apply to survivor benefits and spousal benefits. If you receive survivors benefits, we use your full retirement age for retirement benefits when applying the annual earnings test (AET) for retirement or survivors benefits. Although the full retirement age for survivors benefits may be earlier, for AET purposes, we use your full retirement age for retirement benefits.

Reporting Requirements

You must report all your earnings to us. When you apply for Social Security benefits while still working, you'll need to estimate your annual earnings. If your actual earnings differ significantly from your estimate, you must report changes promptly by calling 1-800-772-1213. Failure to report accurately can result in overpayments that you'll need to repay later.

International Work Considerations

Different rules apply if you work outside the United States while receiving Social Security benefits. If you are younger than full retirement age at any time in 2025, and you are working outside the United States, you must tell us. Your work may affect your benefits under different criteria than domestic earnings tests.

The Annual Earnings Test: Limits and Penalties

The annual earnings test imposes specific dollar limits on how much you can earn while receiving Social Security benefits before your full retirement age. Understanding these limits and their consequences helps you plan your work and benefit claiming strategy effectively.

2025 Earnings Limits

For 2025, two different earnings limits apply depending on your proximity to full retirement age:

If you're under full retirement age for the entire year, the annual earnings limit is $23,400. If you will reach full retirement age in 2025, the limit on your earnings for the months before full retirement age is $62,160.

These limits are adjusted annually for cost-of-living increases, making it important to check current year limits when planning your earnings and benefits strategy.

The Reduction Formula

The consequences of exceeding these limits follow specific mathematical formulas:

For those under full retirement age all year: If you are under full retirement age for the entire year, we deduct $1 from your benefit payments for every $2 you earn above the annual limit. For 2025, that limit is $23,400.

For the year you reach full retirement age: In the year you reach full retirement age, we deduct $1 in benefits for every $3 you earn above a different limit. In 2025, this limit on your earnings is $62,160. We only count your earnings up to the month before you reach your full retirement age, not your earnings for the entire year.

Practical Examples

Let's examine how these formulas work in practice:

Example 1 - Under FRA All Year: You are receiving Social Security retirement benefits every month in 2025 and you are under full retirement age all year. You are entitled to $800 a month in benefits ($9,600 for the year). You work and earn $32,320 ($8,920 more than the $23,400 limit) during the year. Your Social Security benefits would be reduced by $4,460 ($1 for every $2 you earned more than the limit). You would receive $5,140 of your $9,600 in benefits for the year.

Example 2 - Reaching FRA During the Year: You reach full retirement age in August 2025. You are entitled to $800 per month in benefits. From January through July, you're entitled to $5,600 in benefits. You earn $63,000 from January through July ($840 more than the $62,160 limit for those reaching FRA). Your Social Security benefits would be reduced through July by $280 ($1 for every $3 you earned more than the limit). You would still receive $5,320 out of your $5,600 benefits for the first 7 months. Beginning in August 2025 when you reach full retirement age, you would receive your full benefit ($800 per month), no matter how much you earn.

Monthly vs. Annual Testing

While the earnings test is typically applied annually, Social Security uses monthly testing in certain situations, particularly during your first year of retirement. This can be advantageous if you retire mid-year after earning substantial income earlier in the year.

Administration and Timing

Social Security doesn't immediately reduce your benefits when you exceed earnings limits. Instead, they typically review your earnings after the end of the year when your employer reports your actual wages. If you've been overpaid, you'll need to repay the excess, or if you've been underpaid due to conservative earnings estimates, you'll receive additional payments.

Active vs. Passive Income: What Counts?

Understanding which types of income count toward the earnings test is crucial for planning your work and investment strategy while receiving Social Security benefits. The distinction between "earned" and "unearned" income determines whether your Social Security benefits will be affected.

What Counts as Earnings

When we figure out how much to deduct from your benefits, we count only the wages you make from your job or your net profit if you're self-employed. We include bonuses, commissions, and vacation pay in this calculation.

Specifically, earned income includes:

- Wages and salaries from employment
- Net earnings from self-employment
- Bonuses and commissions
- Vacation pay and sick pay
- Back pay and retroactive wage payments (if earned during the benefit year)

What Doesn't Count

The Social Security Administration explicitly excludes numerous income sources from the earnings test:

We don't count pensions, annuities, investment income, interest, veterans benefits, or other government or military retirement benefits. This exclusion list also includes:

- Social Security benefits themselves
- Unemployment benefits
- Workers' compensation
- Investment dividends and capital gains
- Interest from savings accounts, CDs, and bonds
- Rental income from real estate (if you're not actively involved in management)
- IRA and 401(k) distributions
- Pension payments from previous employers

The Self-Employment Complexity

Self-employment income requires more nuanced evaluation. If you're self-employed, we consider only your net earnings from self-employment. However, the timing of when self-employment income is "earned" versus when it's received can affect how it's counted.

For self-employed individuals, the earnings test also considers the substantial services test. You're considered to be working in self-employment if you perform substantial services in your business. This generally means working more than 45 hours per month, or between 15 and 45 hours per month in a highly skilled occupation.

Timing of Income Recognition

Income earned before starting to receive Social Security does not count either. This could include stock options, back pay, bonuses and payments for unused vacation or sick leave. Even if these payments arrive after starting to receive benefits, they aren't included against the earnings limit as long as they were earned before benefits started.

This timing rule can be particularly valuable for people who retire mid-year with substantial income earned earlier in the year before claiming Social Security.

Investment Income Strategies

Since passive investment income doesn't count toward earnings limits, retirees can potentially earn unlimited amounts from properly structured investments without affecting their Social Security benefits. This includes:

- Dividend income from stocks
- Interest from bonds and savings accounts
- Capital gains from selling investments
- Rental income from real estate (with proper management structure)
- Royalty payments from intellectual property

However, you must be careful not to be actively involved in managing these investments to the extent that it becomes self-employment income.

Strategies for Early Retirees Under Full Retirement Age

For people who claim Social Security before reaching full retirement age but want to continue some level of work, several strategies can help maximize benefits while minimizing earnings test impacts.

The Special Earnings Rule

If you retire mid-year, you may already have earned more than the annual earnings limit ($23,400 in 2025). That's why there is a special rule that may apply the first year of retirement. The special rule lets us pay a full Social Security check for any whole month we consider you retired, regardless of your yearly earnings.

For 2025, you are considered retired in any month that:

- If you're under full retirement age all year: your earnings are $1,950 or less and you did not perform substantial services in self-employment
- If you reach full retirement age in 2025: your earnings are $5,180 or less and you did not perform substantial services in self-employment

This rule can be extremely valuable for people who worked full-time earning high wages for part of the year, then retired and took a part-time job with much lower monthly earnings.

Strategic Timing of Retirement

The special earnings rule creates opportunities for strategic retirement timing. Consider someone who earns $60,000 in the first six months of the year, then retires and takes a part-time job earning $1,500 per month. Despite exceeding the annual limit significantly, they could receive full Social Security benefits for each month their earnings stay below the monthly threshold.

Income Timing Strategies

Several timing strategies can help minimize earnings test impacts:

Delay Income Recognition: If possible, delay receiving bonuses, commissions, or other variable compensation until after retirement or until you reach full retirement age.

Structured Self-Employment: If you continue working as a consultant or freelancer, structure your services to avoid the "substantial services" threshold that would count as current earnings.

Investment Timing: Since investment income doesn't count toward earnings limits, consider timing the sale of investments to occur after claiming Social Security rather than taking employment income.

Seasonal Work Strategies

The monthly earnings test can benefit people who work seasonally or have irregular income patterns. For example, a teacher who retires mid-year but continues substitute teaching occasionally might stay below monthly thresholds even if their annual total would exceed the yearly limit.

Health Insurance Considerations

Many early retirees continue working primarily to maintain employer health insurance until Medicare eligibility at 65. Understanding how to structure this continued employment to minimize Social Security benefit impacts while maintaining necessary health coverage requires careful planning.

Spouse Coordination

For married couples, coordinating the timing of Social Security claims and continued work between spouses can optimize overall household benefits. One spouse might continue working while the other claims benefits, or both might work part-time to stay below earnings thresholds.

Getting Your Withheld Benefits Back

Perhaps the most misunderstood aspect of the Social Security earnings test is that withheld benefits aren't lost forever—they're returned to you with interest in the form of higher monthly payments once you reach full retirement age.

The Recalculation Process

If we withhold some of your benefits due to your earnings, your benefit amount will increase when you reach FRA. At full retirement age, Social Security recalculates your benefit to account for the months when benefits were withheld due to the earnings test.

This recalculation effectively treats you as if you had delayed claiming Social Security for those months when benefits were withheld. While you don't receive the full delayed retirement credits that come with voluntarily postponing benefits past full retirement age, you do receive actuarial increases that partially compensate for the withheld benefits.

Automatic Benefit Increases

Your earnings from work may also increase your monthly amount. Each year we automatically review the records for everyone getting benefits who work. If your latest year of earnings are one of your highest years, we'll refigure your benefit and pay you any increase you are due.

This dual benefit means that continuing to work while receiving Social Security can increase your benefits in two ways: through the recalculation of withheld benefits and through higher lifetime earnings that increase your primary insurance amount.

Timeline for Adjustments

The recalculation of your benefits due to withheld payments typically occurs automatically when you reach full retirement age. You don't need to take any action to receive these increased payments—Social Security will adjust your benefits automatically.

However, if your earnings during a year while receiving benefits represent one of your highest 35 years of earnings, that recalculation may take additional time as Social Security reviews your complete earnings record.

Mathematical Impact

The mathematical impact of the benefit recalculation depends on how many months of benefits were withheld and your age when you first claimed benefits. Generally, the younger you are when you first claim benefits, the more significant the percentage increase in your monthly benefit will be when withheld benefits are restored.

For example, someone who claimed benefits at 62 and had benefits withheld for two years due to earnings would receive a more substantial percentage increase in their monthly benefit than someone who claimed at 65 and had benefits withheld for six months.

Long-term Financial Perspective

From a lifetime benefit perspective, the earnings test and subsequent benefit restoration generally don't result in a permanent loss of Social Security income. However, there is an opportunity cost in the form of foregone investment returns on the withheld benefit payments, and the restored benefits don't include interest for the delay.

Planning Implications

Understanding that withheld benefits will be restored should influence your decision-making about working while receiving Social Security. If you need current income and can earn significantly more than the earnings limit, it might make sense to continue working despite temporary benefit reductions, knowing that your monthly payments will increase later.

Record Keeping

While Social Security handles the recalculation automatically, it's wise to keep records of your earnings and any benefit withholdings. This documentation can be helpful if you need to verify that your benefit recalculation was processed correctly when you reach full retirement age.

The earnings test represents a complex but manageable aspect of Social Security planning. By understanding how it works, what income counts, and how to optimize your strategy, you can make informed decisions about when to claim benefits and how to structure your work and investment income during the transition to full retirement. The key insight is that the earnings test is generally a cash flow timing issue rather than a permanent reduction in lifetime benefits, making it possible to work productively while receiving Social Security with proper planning and understanding of the rules.

CHAPTER 9: IRMAA - WHEN HIGHER INCOME MEANS HIGHER MEDICARE COSTS

Of all Medicare's complexities, perhaps none is more frustrating than discovering you'll pay significantly more for the exact same coverage as your neighbor—simply because you were successful in saving for retirement. The Income-Related Monthly Adjustment Amount, better known as IRMAA, represents Medicare's approach to means-testing, where higher-income beneficiaries subsidize the program for others while receiving identical benefits.

IRMAA affects roughly 7% of Medicare beneficiaries, but its impact on retirement planning extends far beyond those currently paying it. Understanding IRMAA's mechanics, thresholds, and strategies to minimize its impact is crucial for anyone with substantial retirement savings, ongoing investment income, or plans for Roth conversions. The two-year lookback period means decisions you make today at age 63 will determine your Medicare costs at age 65, making IRMAA planning an essential component of comprehensive retirement strategy.

What is IRMAA and Who Pays It?

IRMAA stands for Income-Related Monthly Adjustment Amount—a surcharge that higher-income Medicare beneficiaries must pay in addition to standard Medicare Part B and Part D premiums. Implemented as part of the Medicare Modernization Act, IRMAA represents a departure from Medicare's traditional community rating structure, where everyone paid the same premiums regardless of income.

The Basic Framework

The theory behind IRMAA is that higher-income beneficiaries can afford to pay more for their healthcare. Instead of maintaining the standard 25:75 cost-sharing split between beneficiaries and the government, higher-income individuals must pay a larger share of Medicare's costs. The Social Security Administration (SSA) determines your IRMAA eligibility and amount, making it one of the few aspects of Medicare administration handled outside the Centers for Medicare & Medicaid Services.

IRMAA applies to both Medicare Part B (medical insurance covering doctor visits and outpatient services) and Medicare Part D (prescription drug coverage). Importantly, this surcharge affects all Medicare beneficiaries subject to it, whether they're enrolled in Original Medicare with a Medigap policy or a Medicare Advantage plan.

The Two-Year Lookback Rule

Perhaps IRMAA's most challenging aspect is its two-year lookback period for income determination. IRMAA calculations have a two-year lag time. Whether you pay an IRMAA in 2025 depends on the income shown on your 2023 tax returns. This timing creates significant planning challenges because life circumstances can change dramatically between the income year and the Medicare payment year.

The lookback period means that income from age 63 determines your Medicare costs at age 65—before you're even eligible for Medicare. This timing particularly affects people who retire between these ages, as they may pay IRMAA based on their peak earning years despite having much lower current income.

Who Actually Pays IRMAA?

According to the Medicare Trustees Report, about 4.9 million Medicare beneficiaries paid Part B IRMAA surcharges in 2024, amounting to about 7% of the 67 million total enrollees. About 4.2 million beneficiaries paid IRMAA surcharges for their Part D prescription drug coverage. The discrepancy occurs because more beneficiaries have Part B than Part D coverage.

While 7% might seem small, IRMAA's reach is growing. The income thresholds are indexed to inflation, but they don't account for the general increase in retirement account balances among baby boomers. As more people reach retirement with substantial 401(k) and IRA balances, required minimum distributions increasingly push retirees into IRMAA territory.

Modified Adjusted Gross Income (MAGI) Calculation

IRMAA uses Modified Adjusted Gross Income (MAGI) rather than standard Adjusted Gross Income. For IRMAA purposes, MAGI includes:

- Your adjusted gross income from line 11 of Form 1040
- Tax-exempt interest income (municipal bonds, etc.)
- Interest from U.S. savings bonds used for education expenses
- Income earned abroad that was excluded from gross income
- Nontaxable income from U.S. territories

This expanded definition means that many sources of income traditionally considered "tax-free" still count toward IRMAA calculations, creating surprises for retirees who thought they'd structured their finances to minimize taxable income.

Income Thresholds and Surcharge Amounts

Understanding IRMAA's income brackets and corresponding surcharges is essential for retirement planning, as these thresholds create "cliff effects" where crossing an income threshold by even $1 can result in hundreds or thousands of dollars in additional Medicare premiums.

2025 Income Thresholds

For 2025, the IRMAA thresholds are:

Individual Filers:

- $106,000 or less: No IRMAA (standard premiums only)
- $106,001 - $133,000: First IRMAA tier
- $133,001 - $167,000: Second IRMAA tier
- $167,001 - $200,000: Third IRMAA tier
- $200,001 - $500,000: Fourth IRMAA tier
- Above $500,000: Maximum IRMAA tier

Married Filing Jointly:

- $212,000 or less: No IRMAA
- $212,001 - $266,000: First IRMAA tier
- $266,001 - $334,000: Second IRMAA tier
- $334,001 - $400,000: Third IRMAA tier
- $400,001 - $750,000: Fourth IRMAA tier
- Above $750,000: Maximum IRMAA tier

Part B Surcharge Amounts for 2025

The standard Medicare Part B premium is $185 monthly in 2025. IRMAA surcharges add the following amounts:

- First tier: $74.00 monthly (total premium: $259.00)
- Second tier: $185.00 monthly (total premium: $370.00)
- Third tier: $296.00 monthly (total premium: $481.00)
- Fourth tier: $406.30 monthly (total premium: $591.30)
- Fifth tier: $443.90 monthly (total premium: $628.90)

Part D Surcharge Amounts for 2025

Part D IRMAA surcharges are added to your plan's premium:

- First tier: $13.70 monthly
- Second tier: $35.20 monthly
- Third tier: $56.60 monthly
- Fourth tier: $78.10 monthly
- Fifth tier: $85.50 monthly

The Cliff Effect

IRMAA operates as a "cliff" surcharge rather than a gradual increase. This means if your modified adjusted gross income exceeds the threshold by as little as one dollar, you'll have to pay higher premiums. For example, a married couple with exactly $212,000 in MAGI pays standard premiums, while a couple with $212,001 pays an additional $1,052.40 annually ($888 for Part B and $164.40 for Part D) if both are on Medicare.

Married Filing Separately

The thresholds for married individuals filing separately are particularly punitive, essentially treating each spouse as if they had the single filer income limits regardless of their actual income split. This filing status rarely provides IRMAA advantages and often results in higher surcharges than filing jointly.

Annual Adjustments

The first four IRMAA brackets are adjusted annually for inflation using the Consumer Price Index for Urban Consumers (CPI-U). However, the fifth bracket (highest income tier) is currently frozen and cannot be indexed for inflation until 2028. This means the highest earners face a gradually increasing effective tax rate as inflation erodes the real value of the top threshold.

Life-Changing Events and Appeals Process

One of IRMAA's most taxpayer-friendly features is the appeals process that allows beneficiaries to use more recent income information when they've experienced significant life changes that reduced their income.

Qualifying Life-Changing Events

The Social Security Administration recognizes seven specific life-changing events that can justify using more recent income information:

1. Marriage - Getting married can change your filing status and potentially reduce per-person IRMAA liability

2. Divorce or annulment - May significantly reduce household income and IRMAA exposure

3. Death of spouse - Often results in substantial income reduction

4. Work stoppage - Retirement or involuntary job loss

5. Work reduction - Significant reduction in work hours or self-employment income

6. Loss of income-producing property - Due to natural disaster, disease, fraud, or other circumstances beyond your control

7. Employer settlement payment - Due to employer closure, bankruptcy, or reorganization

The Appeal Process Using Form SSA-44

To request reconsideration based on a life-changing event, you must complete Form SSA-44 (Medicare Income-Related Monthly Adjustment Amount – Life-Changing Event). This form requires detailed information about your situation and supporting documentation.

The appeal process involves several steps:

1. Complete Form SSA-44 with accurate income projections and life event details

2. Gather supporting documentation such as retirement letters, death certificates, divorce decrees, or employer statements

3. Submit to Social Security via mail, fax, or in-person visit to a local office

4. Provide income estimates for the current year and potentially future years

Documentation Requirements

Different life events require specific supporting documentation:

- Retirement: Letter from employer confirming retirement date, plus tax returns showing reduced income
- Death of spouse: Death certificate and tax returns showing income change
- Divorce: Final divorce decree and documentation of income division
- Work reduction: Employer letter confirming reduced hours or responsibilities
- Natural disaster: FEMA declaration or insurance documentation

Timing and Retroactive Relief

Appeals can be filed at any time after receiving an IRMAA determination notice, but it's advantageous to file as early as possible. If approved, the adjustment applies retroactively to January 1 of the year in question. If IRMAA surcharges were deducted from Social Security benefits, you'll receive refund payments.

Importantly, submitting Form SSA-44 is not technically an "appeal"—it's a request for a new initial determination based on more recent information. This distinction matters because the process is generally simpler and more likely to succeed than formal appeals of coverage decisions.

Success Rates and Expectations

Life-changing event requests are generally successful when properly documented and the event genuinely resulted in reduced income. However, certain situations don't qualify:

- Voluntary large distributions or Roth conversions (these are considered choices, not life-changing events)
- Investment losses that don't affect MAGI
- Changes in expenses that don't affect income
- Temporary income fluctuations without permanent changes

Multiple Level Appeals

If your initial life-changing event request is denied, you can pursue additional levels of appeal:

1. Reconsideration by Social Security Administration

2. Administrative Law Judge hearing through the Office of Medicare Hearings and Appeals

3. Medicare Appeals Council review

4. Federal district court appeal

Most IRMAA appeals resolve at the initial or reconsideration level, making formal hearings relatively rare.

Tax Strategies to Minimize IRMAA

Effective IRMAA planning requires a multi-year tax strategy that considers not just current year income optimization, but the two-year lookback period and the interplay between various income sources and Medicare costs.

Income Timing and Smoothing

The most fundamental IRMAA strategy involves timing income recognition to stay below thresholds or minimize time spent in higher brackets. This requires planning at least three years in advance due to the two-year lookback period.

Strategic Retirement Timing: If you're planning to retire, the timing can significantly impact IRMAA. Retiring in January allows you to potentially qualify for a life-changing event appeal, while retiring mid-year might result in high IRMAA payments based on partial-year high earnings followed by lower retirement income.

Capital Gains Management: Since capital gains are included in MAGI, timing asset sales becomes crucial. Consider spreading large gains over multiple years rather than recognizing them all in a single year that might trigger IRMAA.

Investment Income Optimization

Several investment strategies can help minimize IRMAA exposure:

Municipal Bond Strategy: While tax-exempt municipal bond interest counts toward IRMAA MAGI, the after-tax analysis might still favor munis for high-income retirees. The key is understanding that "tax-free" doesn't mean "IRMAA-free."

Tax-Loss Harvesting: Realizing investment losses to offset gains becomes more valuable when IRMAA is considered, as the effective marginal tax rate includes both income taxes and Medicare surcharge increases.

Roth IRA Distributions: Once assets are in Roth accounts, distributions don't count toward MAGI, making Roth IRAs particularly valuable for IRMAA planning.

Qualified Charitable Distribution (QCD): For those over 70½, making charitable contributions directly from IRAs through QCDs reduces both taxable income and IRMAA exposure. You can donate up to $100,000 annually without the distribution counting toward MAGI.

Required Minimum Distribution Planning

Since Required Minimum Distributions (RMDs) begin at age 73 and often push retirees into IRMAA territory, advance planning becomes crucial:

Pre-RMD Roth Conversions: Converting traditional IRA assets to Roth IRAs before RMDs begin can reduce future mandatory distributions and IRMAA exposure.

Asset Location Strategy: Positioning high-growth investments in Roth accounts and more conservative assets in traditional accounts can reduce future RMD amounts.

Charitable Remainder Trusts: For significant IRA balances, charitable remainder trusts can provide income while reducing IRMAA exposure through charitable deductions.

Health Savings Account Optimization

For those still working with access to HSAs, maximizing contributions provides triple tax benefits: deductible contributions, tax-free growth, and tax-free qualified withdrawals that don't count toward IRMAA calculations.

Social Security Timing Strategy

Delaying Social Security benefits until age 70 serves multiple purposes: benefits grow at 8% annually, and the delayed benefits don't count toward IRMAA during the delay period. This can be particularly valuable for high earners who would otherwise face significant IRMAA surcharges.

Business and Self-Employment Planning

Small business owners have additional IRMAA planning opportunities:

Income Acceleration/Deferral: Business owners can sometimes control when income is recognized through timing of sales, collections, or business structure changes.

Retirement Plan Contributions: Maximizing SEP-IRA or Solo 401(k) contributions can reduce current MAGI while building retirement assets.

Equipment Purchases: Section 179 deductions and bonus depreciation can reduce business income in years when IRMAA avoidance is crucial.

Roth Conversions and Medicare Costs

Roth IRA conversions represent perhaps the most powerful long-term strategy for IRMAA avoidance, but they require careful timing and analysis to avoid triggering IRMAA in the conversion year while providing future benefits.

The Roth Conversion Paradox

Roth conversions create a fundamental timing dilemma: converting assets to avoid future IRMAA often triggers IRMAA in the conversion year. This paradox requires sophisticated analysis to determine whether the short-term IRMAA cost is justified by long-term benefits.

When you convert traditional IRA or 401(k) assets to a Roth IRA, the converted amount is treated as taxable income in the conversion year. This income counts toward IRMAA calculations, potentially pushing you into higher Medicare premium brackets.

Strategic Timing for Roth Conversions

The optimal timing for Roth conversions depends on your Medicare enrollment timeline and income patterns:

Ages 60-62: Generally the safest time for large conversions since this income won't affect Medicare premiums that begin at 65 (due to the two-year lookback period).

Age 63+: Requires careful analysis since conversion income will affect Medicare premiums. However, conversions might still be beneficial if they prevent larger IRMAA exposure from future RMDs.

Post-Medicare Enrollment: Conversions remain valuable but require year-by-year IRMAA analysis to optimize timing.

Roth Conversion Amount Optimization

Rather than converting entire traditional IRA balances at once, consider systematic conversions that maximize tax bracket utilization while managing IRMAA exposure:

Bracket Management: Convert amounts that fill up your current tax bracket without crossing IRMAA thresholds. For example, if you're in the 22% tax bracket but below the first IRMAA tier, convert enough to reach the IRMAA threshold but not exceed it.

Multi-Year Strategy: Spread conversions over several years to avoid large income spikes that trigger high IRMAA tiers. This approach often provides better overall tax efficiency even if it triggers some IRMAA years.

IRMAA Break-Even Analysis

Determining whether Roth conversions make sense despite IRMAA requires comparing:

1. Conversion Year Costs: Additional income taxes plus IRMAA surcharges

2. Future Benefits: Reduced RMDs, eliminated future IRMAA from those distributions, and tax-free Roth withdrawals

3. Time Value: Present value calculations considering investment growth and inflation

For most high-income retirees, the analysis favors Roth conversions despite short-term IRMAA increases, particularly when conversions are done systematically over multiple years.

Conversion Timing Within the Year

For those age 63 and older contemplating Roth conversions, consider doing conversions in November or December. By this time, you'll have a clear picture of your total income for the year and can optimize the conversion amount to manage IRMAA exposure.

Roth Conversion and Life-Changing Events

One sophisticated strategy involves timing Roth conversions around qualifying life-changing events. For example, if you retire mid-year, you might:

1. Do a large Roth conversion in the retirement year

2. File a life-changing event appeal to reduce IRMAA based on your reduced post-retirement income

3. Use the appeal process to avoid IRMAA on the conversion income

However, this strategy requires careful documentation and isn't guaranteed to succeed.

Long-Term IRMAA Avoidance Strategy

The ultimate goal of Roth conversions for IRMAA planning is creating a retirement income structure that minimizes IRMAA exposure:

Asset Location Optimization: Having substantial Roth assets allows you to control taxable income in retirement by choosing whether to take distributions from taxable, tax-deferred, or tax-free accounts.

Flexible Withdrawal Strategy: With assets in multiple account types, you can adjust withdrawal patterns to stay below IRMAA thresholds in years when Medicare premiums are particularly important.

Estate Planning Benefits: Roth assets also provide estate planning advantages since beneficiaries inherit tax-free assets without RMD requirements (under current law).

Medicare Advantage Considerations

Even if you choose Medicare Advantage plans to potentially reduce overall healthcare costs, you're still subject to IRMAA surcharges on Part B and Part D premiums. This means IRMAA planning remains important regardless of your Medicare plan choice.

Understanding and planning for IRMAA requires a comprehensive approach that considers not just current tax minimization, but the long-term interplay between retirement income, Medicare costs, and overall financial strategy. The two-year lookback period makes IRMAA planning particularly challenging, but also provides opportunities for sophisticated tax and retirement planning that can save thousands of dollars annually in Medicare premiums while optimizing overall retirement income strategies.

CHAPTER 10: LONG-TERM CARE AND MEDICAID PLANNING

When Eleanor and Frank celebrated their 40th wedding anniversary in their cozy two-bedroom home, they never imagined that five years later, Frank's Alzheimer's diagnosis would force them to navigate one of the most complex and emotionally challenging aspects of retirement planning: long-term care. Like millions of American couples, they discovered that the healthcare safety nets they thought they understood—Medicare and traditional health insurance—offered little protection against the devastating financial impact of extended care needs. Eleanor found herself facing the terrifying prospect of not only losing her husband to a cruel disease but also potentially losing their home, their life savings, and her own financial security in the process.

This scenario plays out in countless households across America every day. The statistics are sobering: close to 70% of people turning 65 today will need long-term care at some point in their life, yet most people remain woefully unprepared for this reality. The misconception that Medicare will cover long-term care needs is perhaps one of the most dangerous financial assumptions that retirees make. Understanding the limitations of Medicare coverage, the complexities of Medicaid planning, and the various strategies available to protect your assets and your spouse requires careful planning that ideally begins years before care is actually needed. This chapter will guide you through these critical considerations, helping you develop a comprehensive strategy that protects both your health and your wealth.

Medicare's Limited Long-Term Care Coverage

The harsh reality that surprises many retirees is just how limited Medicare's coverage is when it comes to long-term care needs. Medicare does not provide long-term care coverage or custodial care unless medical care is needed. This distinction between medical care and custodial care is crucial to understand, as it forms the foundation of Medicare's coverage limitations.

Medicare Part A will cover skilled nursing facility care, but only under very specific and restrictive conditions. You must have Part A and have days left in your benefit period to use, have a qualifying inpatient hospital stay, enter the SNF within a short time (generally 30 days) of leaving the hospital, and your doctor must decide that you need daily skilled care. The qualifying hospital stay must be at least three consecutive days as an inpatient, not counting the day of discharge.

Even when these strict criteria are met, Medicare's coverage is severely limited in both duration and scope. Days 1 – 20: Nothing, Days 21 – 100: $209.50 each day, Days 101 and beyond: You pay all costs. This means that Medicare provides full coverage for only the first 20 days of skilled nursing care, partial coverage for days 21-100 with significant daily copayments, and absolutely no coverage beyond 100 days.

The definition of "skilled care" further restricts Medicare coverage. Most long-term care isn't medical care. Instead, most long-term care helps with basic personal tasks of everyday life, sometimes called "activities of daily living." This may include: Help with personal care assistance (like dressing, bathing, and using the bathroom). These activities of daily living, while essential for quality of life and safety, are not considered medical care under Medicare's definition.

Medicare will cover some home health services, but again with significant limitations. Medicare will cover part-time skilled nursing care, physical therapy, occupational therapy and other skilled care services provided in your home if you meet certain conditions. However, this coverage is typically short-term and does not include 24-hour care, meal delivery, or help with activities of daily living like bathing and dressing.

For those facing terminal illnesses, Medicare does provide comprehensive hospice coverage, which includes medical care, prescription drugs for symptom control, and support services for patients and their families. However, this coverage is specifically designed for end-of-life care rather than long-term custodial care needs.

Understanding these limitations is critical because relying solely on Medicare for long-term care needs is not a viable strategy for most retirees. The gap between what people expect Medicare to cover and what it actually covers represents one of the largest potential financial risks in retirement planning.

Medicaid Estate Recovery: Protecting Your Assets

While Medicaid does cover long-term care costs for those who qualify financially, it comes with a significant catch that many families don't discover until it's too late: the Medicaid Estate Recovery Program (MERP). After a Medicaid Long Term Care beneficiary dies, the Medicaid Estate Recovery Program (MERP) in their state is required by law to seek reimbursement for their Medicaid long-term care expenses.

This federal requirement means that State Medicaid programs must recover certain Medicaid benefits paid on behalf of a Medicaid enrollee. For individuals age 55 or older, states are required to seek recovery of payments from the individual's estate for nursing facility services, home and community-based services, and related hospital and prescription drug services.

The scope of estate recovery varies by state, but it can be extensive. This Medicaid clawback includes the costs of nursing home care, in-home care provided through Home and Community Based Services (HCBS) Waivers or Aged, Blind and Disabled Medicaid, and any prescription drug or hospitalization costs related to long-term care. Some states go even further and attempt to recover costs for all Medicaid services, not just long-term care.

For most families, the home represents the largest asset subject to estate recovery. When someone has been on Medicaid at the end of their life, the home is usually the last remaining thing of value after death, so states will attempt recovery via the home. However, there are important protections and exemptions built into the system.

Federal law provides certain deferrals that temporarily protect estates from recovery. States may not recover from the estate of a deceased Medicaid enrollee who is survived by a spouse, child under age 21, or blind or disabled child of any age. These protections are typically temporary—once these conditions no longer exist, recovery may proceed.

States also vary in their minimum thresholds for pursuing recovery. Some states won't use MERP if the home is valued below a certain amount. Texas, for example, does not try to be reimbursed from a recipient whose estate is valued below $10,000, while Georgia's limit is $25,000. Additionally, Estates with a gross value of $25,000 or less are exempt from estate recovery in Georgia, with the state waiving claims against the first $25,000 of any estate.

The method of estate recovery also varies significantly. With MERP, all states are required to seek recovery from the deceased Medicaid recipient's "probate estate". However, States also have the option to attempt recovery from assets that do not go through probate. This is known as an "expanded" definition of estate recovery and includes assets that are jointly held other than "tenants in common", life estates, and assets in a living trust.

Understanding your state's specific recovery rules is crucial for effective planning. States that only pursue probate estate recovery offer more planning opportunities than those with expanded recovery powers. For probate-only states, simply keeping assets out of probate will protect them from Estate Recovery.

Hardship waivers provide another potential protection. States are also required to establish procedures for waiving estate recovery when recovery would cause an undue hardship. The heirs would need financial help from the government if the state filed a MERP claim to get money back is one example of a hardship situation that might qualify for a waiver.

Long-Term Care Insurance Options

Given Medicare's limitations and Medicaid's estate recovery requirements, long-term care insurance emerges as a critical component of comprehensive retirement planning. The insurance landscape offers several different approaches to coverage, each with distinct advantages and considerations.

Traditional long-term care insurance policies provide dedicated coverage specifically designed for long-term care needs. According to the 2024 American Association for Long-Term Care Insurance (AALTCI) annual Price Index survey, the average annual premium for a $165,000-benefit policy with no inflation protection is $950 for a single male (age 55) and $1,500 for a single female (age 55). The cost differential between men and women reflects actuarial data showing that women typically live longer and are more likely to need extended care.

Age significantly impacts premium costs, making early purchase advantageous. When the same long-term care insurance policy is purchased at age 60, premiums rise. The average annual premium for a single male is $1,200 and $1,900 for a single female. Couples can expect to pay around $2,600 for a combined yearly premium. This represents a substantial increase in just five years, highlighting the importance of obtaining coverage while younger and healthier.

For 2025, premium ranges vary considerably based on coverage levels and features. In 2025, you can expect to pay anywhere from $79 to $533 per month for a long-term care insurance policy. These premiums, however, vary greatly based on age, gender, health, and the coverage amount of the policy.

Several factors influence long-term care insurance costs beyond age and gender. Type of policy: Traditional long-term care insurance policies may be priced differently than hybrid policies. Coverage amount and duration: Premiums increase with more comprehensive coverages and a longer benefit period. Elimination period: This refers to the waiting period before benefits kick in, with lower premiums for longer periods. Inflation protection: Adding inflation protection ensures that benefits keep pace with rising care costs, but it also increases the monthly premium.

Hybrid policies represent an increasingly popular alternative that combines long-term care benefits with life insurance or annuity features. One type of hybrid insurance offers life insurance and long-term care. A single policy that provides benefits for two different scenarios can be very efficient. You have long-term care coverage available for you, and your beneficiaries receive a life insurance death benefit if you pass away before needing it. If long-term care is needed, policyholders can accelerate the death benefit to pay for care, with additional coverage available even after the death benefit is exhausted.

Another hybrid option involves long-term care annuities. Another type of hybrid is a long-term care annuity, which provides long-term care insurance at a multiple of the initial investment amount. The investment grows tax-free at a fixed rate of return, and, if used for long-term care expenses, gains will be received income tax-free. However, current interest rate environments have limited the availability and attractiveness of these products.

Tax benefits make long-term care insurance more affordable for many people. Attained Age Before Close of Taxable Year 2025 Limit: 40 or less $480, More than 40 but not more than 50 $900, More than 50 but not more than 60 $1,800, More than 60 but not more than 70 $4,810, More than 70 $6,020. These amounts represent the maximum annual premiums that can be deducted as qualified medical expenses, subject to the overall limitation that medical expenses must exceed 7.5% of adjusted gross income.

The rising costs of long-term care make insurance coverage increasingly valuable. Data from the Centers for Medicare & Medicaid Services shows that assisted living facility costs are projected to increase by 4.7% annually until 2030, while home health care costs are expected to rise by an average of 7% per year. These inflation rates significantly outpace general inflation, making inflation protection riders particularly important for younger purchasers.

State Partnership Programs offer an additional incentive for purchasing long-term care insurance. If your state offers one, you may also be able to get long-term care insurance through a state partnership program. These programs allow you to purchase a shorter-term policy. Then, if you exhaust your benefits, you can potentially qualify for Medicaid assistance and still protect a portion of your assets.

Protecting the Family Home

For most American families, the home represents their largest asset and holds significant emotional value beyond its financial worth. For many West Virginia families, the family home is more than just a property. It represents years of hard work, financial stability, and memories that span generations. However, this cherished asset faces potential risk from Medicaid estate recovery if proper planning isn't implemented.

The home enjoys certain protections during the Medicaid recipient's lifetime, but these protections don't automatically extend after death. Even if the Medicaid applicant were single, there are federal laws in place to protect the home. For instance, if a Medicaid recipient receives home and community based services from Medicaid, but remains living in their home, it would be exempt, but only up to a certain equity interest value.

The primary residence, as long as its equity does not exceed $730,000 (2025 limit) if the applicant or their spouse lives in it, or if the applicant has intent to return to the home, is generally exempt during the applicant's lifetime. However, once the recipient passes away and exemptions no longer apply, Medicaid can place a claim against the home to recover funds.

Several legal strategies can protect the family home from estate recovery while maintaining Medicaid eligibility. Life estate deeds represent one of the most effective protection methods in many states. A life estate deed allows you to transfer ownership of your home to beneficiaries, such as children, while retaining the right to live in and control the property during your lifetime. This strategy removes the home from the probate estate while allowing the original owner to continue living there.

Some states offer specific deed options that provide enhanced protection. For example, in some states, a Ladybird Deed, a type of life estate deed, can be utilized to protect one's home. With this arrangement, the Medicaid beneficiary is the homeowner while living, but upon death, the home automatically transfers to the listed beneficiary, avoiding Estate Recovery. These enhanced life estate deeds, also known as Lady Bird deeds, allow the original owner to retain more control over the property than traditional life estate deeds.

Medicaid Asset Protection Trusts (MAPTs) offer another sophisticated planning tool, though they require advance planning to navigate the five-year look-back period. Trusts serve as an effective tool for shielding assets from Medicaid's reach, especially irrevocable ones like Medicaid Asset Protection Trusts (MAPTs). By placing assets into these trusts, individuals can remove them from personal ownership, keeping them out of Medicaid's asset calculations.

Joint ownership strategies can provide protection in states that only pursue probate estate recovery. However, joint ownership must be structured carefully to avoid unintended consequences. Assets that go through probate include those strictly in the deceased's name, or if jointly owned, ones that are "tenants in common". Joint tenancy with right of survivorship, by contrast, typically passes automatically to the surviving owner outside of probate.

The timing of asset protection planning is crucial due to Medicaid's look-back period. West Virginia has a 60-month (5-year) look-back period for asset transfers. Transfers made within this period can result in penalties that delay Medicaid eligibility, making advance planning essential.

State-specific variations in recovery laws create different planning opportunities and requirements. Understanding whether your state pursues only probate estates or has expanded recovery powers influences the most effective protection strategies. Understanding Medicaid Estate Recovery and Estate

Planning techniques can be complicated, particularly since the rules are not consistent across states. For this reason, it is highly suggested one consult with a Professional Medicaid Planner regarding their particular situation.

Spousal Impoverishment Rules

When one spouse requires long-term care that qualifies for Medicaid coverage, federal law provides important protections to prevent the community spouse (the spouse remaining at home) from becoming impoverished. In 1988, Congress enacted provisions to prevent what has come to be called "spousal impoverishment," leaving the spouse who is still living at home in the community with little or no income or resources.

These protections, known as spousal impoverishment rules, include both income and asset protections. Spousal Impoverishment Rules include a Minimum Monthly Maintenance Needs Allowance (MMMNA) and a Community Spouse Resource Allowance (CSRA) that "protect" a portion of a couple's income and assets (including the home) for the non-applicant spouse.

The Community Spouse Resource Allowance (CSRA) determines how much of the couple's assets the community spouse can retain. Generally speaking, in 2025, the applicant asset limit for a senior is $2,000. Medicaid, however, allows a greater portion of the couple's assets to be protected for the non-applicant spouse. This is the CSRA. The calculation of the CSRA is based on a "snapshot" of the couple's assets taken on a specific date, typically the first day of the applicant's continuous institutionalization for at least 30 days.

The community spouse is allowed to keep a maximum of half (1/2) of the non-exempt assets up to a total of $157,920 (2025) or at least a minimum of $31,584 (2025). This means that in most cases, the community spouse can retain between approximately $31,584 and $157,920 in countable assets, depending on the total value of the couple's assets.

Income protections ensure that the community spouse has adequate monthly income to maintain their household. Minimum Monthly Maintenance Needs Allowance (Effective July 2025 – June 2026) $2,643.75 for all states, but Alaska and Hawaii $3,303.75 in Alaska $3,040.00 in Hawaii. If the community spouse's own income falls below this minimum standard, they can receive additional income from their spouse up to the allowable limit.

The exact amount of the MMMNA varies based on the cost of housing. In 2025, this MMMNA can fall between a minimum of about $2,644/month and a maximum of $3,948/month. The higher allowance may be available when the community spouse has high housing costs or other exceptional circumstances.

The spousal impoverishment protections have been extended beyond nursing home care to include home and community-based services. While the original implementation of Spousal Impoverishment Rules were strictly for non-applicant spouses of Nursing Home Medicaid applicants, in January of 2014, Section 2404 of the Affordable Care Act extended these rules to married couples with one spouse applying for a Home and Community Based Services (HCBS) Medicaid Waiver.

Understanding the calculation methods used in your state is important for maximizing protections. The way this is calculated is based on if a state is a 50% or a 100% state. In 50% states, half of a couple's assets are considered owned by the applicant spouse, and the other half owned by the non-applicant spouse. A community spouse can keep half of the couple's countable assets, up to their state's maximum resource standard.

Planning strategies can help maximize spousal protections while ensuring Medicaid qualification. These might include properly timing asset transfers, structuring income sources, and understanding how different types of assets are treated under spousal impoverishment rules. However, such planning must be done carefully to avoid creating disqualifying transfers or other eligibility issues.

The complexity of spousal impoverishment rules, combined with their interaction with estate recovery provisions, underscores the importance of comprehensive planning that considers both spouses' long-term needs and financial security. Professional guidance from qualified elder law attorneys or certified Medicaid planners becomes essential for navigating these complex rules while maximizing available protections and benefits.

CHAPTER 11: DIVORCE, DEATH, AND MEDICARE/SOCIAL SECURITY

When Margaret received the divorce papers at age 58, her first thought wasn't about splitting assets or custody arrangements—it was about her future healthcare and retirement security. After 23 years of marriage, she suddenly faced questions she'd never considered: Would she still be able to get her ex-husband's Social Security benefits? What would happen to her health insurance? How would Medicare work when she turned 65? Three years later, when her dear friend Susan lost her husband unexpectedly, Margaret watched Susan navigate an equally complex maze of survivor benefits, COBRA deadlines, and Medicare enrollment decisions while grieving the loss of her life partner.

These scenarios represent profound life transitions that millions of Americans face, often at the most emotionally challenging times. The intersection of divorce, death, and federal benefit programs creates a web of rules, deadlines, and opportunities that can significantly impact your financial security for decades to come. Understanding your rights and options before you need them isn't just prudent planning—it's essential protection for your future wellbeing. Whether you're currently married, divorced, widowed, or simply planning ahead, this chapter will guide you through the complex landscape of how major life events affect your Medicare and Social Security benefits, ensuring you're prepared to make informed decisions when life takes unexpected turns.

Divorce and Your Medicare/Social Security Rights

The end of a marriage doesn't necessarily end your eligibility for family benefits, though more than 4 in 10 Americans nearing retirement age do not know that divorced people can collect Social Security benefits based on their ex-spouse's earnings. This widespread lack of awareness can cost divorced individuals thousands of dollars annually in benefits they've rightfully earned through their former marriage.

Understanding divorced spouse Social Security benefits requires meeting specific eligibility criteria that protect the financial security of both parties while preventing abuse of the system. So long as some basic rules are met, you may be eligible to claim a higher retirement benefit based on your ex's work record. The cornerstone requirement is the length of your marriage: You must have been married to your ex-spouse for at least 10 continuous years immediately before the divorce became final.

The 10-year rule serves as the foundation for all divorced spouse benefits, but other critical requirements must also be met. You must be at least 62 years old to claim retirement benefits as a divorced spouse, though claiming before your full retirement age will result in permanently reduced benefits. You can claim as early as 62, but you will get 65% of what you would get at FRA, assuming your FRA is age 67. This reduction is even more severe than for individual benefits, making timing crucial for maximizing your financial security.

Current marital status plays a pivotal role in eligibility. You must be unmarried at the time you apply for and receive divorced spouse benefits. If you remarry, you generally lose eligibility for benefits on your former spouse's record. However, this restriction isn't permanent: if your subsequent marriage ends through divorce, annulment, or death, you may regain eligibility for benefits based on your prior ex-spouse's record.

Your ex-spouse must be entitled to Social Security retirement or disability benefits, meaning they must be at least age 62 or receiving Social Security Disability Insurance. Importantly, Your ex doesn't need to be receiving benefits. This is a key difference from current-spouse benefits. You can get ex-spouse benefits if your former mate hasn't filed for Social Security yet — but only if the divorce is at least 2 years old.

The benefit calculation for divorced spouses mirrors the rules for current spouses. If you qualify as an ex-spouse based on these criteria, your retirement benefit would be half of your ex's primary insurance amount, or PIA, so long as you claim at your full retirement age (FRA). However, you'll only receive the divorced spouse benefit if it exceeds your own retirement benefit based on your earnings record.

One of the most misunderstood aspects of divorced spouse benefits involves their impact on your ex-spouse and their current family. Claiming won't reduce your ex's Social Security benefits or their current spouse's benefits. The Social Security Administration won't notify your ex that you've claimed on their record. This protection ensures that claiming your rightful benefits doesn't create conflict or financial hardship for your former spouse or their new family.

The earnings test applies to divorced spouse benefits just as it does to other Social Security benefits. Like retirement and survivor benefits, spouse and ex-spouse benefits are subject to Social Security's earnings test. If you are below full retirement age and continue to earn income from work, your benefits may be temporarily reduced. In 2025, the earnings test for people who will reach FRA in a later year is $23,400.

For divorced individuals with multiple ex-spouses, the rules provide flexibility while maintaining system integrity. Even if your last divorce doesn't meet the 10-year rule with that specific ex-spouse, you might still qualify based on a previous marriage to a different ex-spouse, provided that earlier marriage lasted at least 10 years before ending in divorce. This provision recognizes that some individuals may have multiple long-term marriages throughout their lives.

Medicare eligibility for divorced individuals operates differently from Social Security, as Medicare is an individual health care plan, not a family plan, so your former spouse's Medicare eligibility does not directly impact your own Medicare eligibility. However, your ex-spouse's work history may help you qualify for premium-free Medicare Part A if you don't have sufficient work credits of your own.

To qualify for Medicare Part A based on your ex-spouse's work record, You were married at least 10 years before the date your divorce was final and your former spouse must have worked and paid Medicare taxes for at least 10 years (40 quarters). This can result in significant savings, as You may pay $518 per month in 2025 if your spouse worked less than 30 quarters but qualify for premium-free Part A through your ex-spouse's work history.

Survivor Benefits: Social Security and Medicare

When a spouse dies, the surviving spouse faces not only emotional devastation but also immediate financial concerns about maintaining their standard of living. Social Security survivor benefits serve as a crucial safety net, with Nearly 3.7 million widows and widowers, including some divorced from late beneficiaries, were receiving survivor benefits as of February 2025.

Survivor benefits represent one of Social Security's most valuable protections, often providing substantially higher monthly payments than spousal benefits during the deceased's lifetime. A surviving spouse can collect 100 percent of the late spouse's benefit if the survivor has reached full retirement age, but the amount will be lower if the deceased spouse claims benefits before reaching full retirement age.

The eligibility requirements for survivor benefits are generally more flexible than those for divorced spouse benefits. In most cases, a widow or widower qualifies for survivor benefits if he or she is at least 60 and was married to the deceased for at least nine months at the time of death. This nine-month requirement has important exceptions that recognize tragic circumstances: if the death was accidental or occurred in military service, there's no length-of-marriage requirement.

Disability and child care provisions provide additional pathways to survivor benefits. You can apply for survivor benefits as early as age 50 if you have a disability that occurred within seven years of your spouse's death. If you care for children from the marriage who are under 16 or have a disability, you can apply at any age.

The timing of when you claim survivor benefits significantly impacts your monthly payment amount. Full retirement age for survivor benefits differs from that for regular retirement benefits, creating important planning considerations. FRA for survivor benefits differs from that for retirement benefits; it's 66 and 4 months if the survivor was born in 1958, 66 and 6 months for those born in 1959 and rises in steps to 67 for those people in 1962 and after.

Claiming survivor benefits before full retirement age results in reduced payments, but the reduction schedule differs from regular retirement benefits. Payments start at 71.5% of your spouse's benefit and increase the longer you wait to apply. Over 75% at age 61. Over 80% at age 63. Over 90% at age 65. You can get up to 100% when you reach your "Full Retirement Age for Survivor benefits".

If the deceased spouse had delayed claiming Social Security beyond their full retirement age, those delayed retirement credits benefit the survivor. If the deceased had passed FRA without claiming Social Security, the survivor benefit will be boosted to reflect the delayed retirement credits they would have earned for putting off filing. This provision ensures that the deceased's strategy to maximize benefits continues to provide value for their surviving spouse.

For surviving spouses who are eligible for both their own retirement benefit and survivor benefits, Social Security provides important flexibility. Social Security doesn't add benefits together. If you're entitled to two types of payments — as both a retiree and a survivor of one, for example — Social Security determines which payment is higher and sends you that amount.

However, survivor benefits enjoy a special exemption from the "deemed filing" rule that applies to spousal benefits. Retirement and spousal benefits are usually subject to a rule called deemed filing: When you claim one, you're deemed to be simultaneously claiming the other if you're eligible for both. That's not the case with survivor benefits. This means you can claim survivor benefits first while allowing your own retirement benefit to grow with delayed retirement credits until age 70.

Divorced spouses can also claim survivor benefits under specific circumstances. The marriage must have lasted at least 10 years, and the surviving divorced spouse must be unmarried (though they can remarry after age 60 without losing eligibility). Divorced people can receive survivor benefits of 71.5 percent to 100 percent of the late former spouse's benefit amount, depending on your age when you claim.

Medicare eligibility for surviving spouses operates based on the deceased spouse's work history, providing crucial healthcare coverage for those who may not have sufficient work credits of their own. If your deceased spouse was eligible for Medicare, you may qualify for premium-free Medicare Part A based on their work record, following the same rules that apply to current spouses.

Children of deceased workers may also qualify for survivor benefits, providing crucial support for families facing the loss of a primary breadwinner. The children of deceased workers may be able to collect survivor benefits of up to 75 percent of what their late parent was getting (or would have been entitled to get) from Social Security. About 2.1 million children were doing so as of February 2025.

Remarriage Considerations

The decision to remarry later in life involves not only emotional considerations but also significant financial implications for Social Security and Medicare benefits. Understanding how remarriage affects your current and future benefit eligibility can influence both the timing of a new marriage and your overall retirement planning strategy.

For those currently receiving divorced spouse benefits, remarriage generally ends eligibility for benefits based on your ex-spouse's record. Divorced spouse's benefits – Generally, if you remarry, benefits paid to you on your former spouse's record stop. You should report your new marriage to us to avoid being overpaid. However, this loss of benefits may be offset by eligibility for spousal benefits based on your new spouse's work record.

The age at which you remarry plays a crucial role in determining its impact on survivor benefits. If you remarry before age 50 – You won't be eligible for survivors or disability benefits as a surviving spouse unless your later marriage ends by divorce or annulment. If you remarry between the ages of 50 and 59 – You may be able to get benefits as a disabled surviving spouse.

For most surviving spouses, the critical threshold is age 60. If the remarriage took place before you turned 60 (50 if you have a disability), you cannot draw survivor benefits. You regain eligibility if that marriage ends. And there is no effect on eligibility for survivor benefits if you remarry at or past those ages. This rule recognizes that older remarriages often involve two individuals with established benefit entitlements from their previous marriages.

When remarriage occurs after the age threshold, you maintain the right to choose the highest benefit available to you. If you were divorced but have since remarried, you are now a spouse from Social Security's perspective. You are no longer an ex-spouse. Your spousal retirement benefits will be based on your current spouse's work history (if eligible), not your ex's, regardless of whether your current or former spouse has a larger primary insurance amount.

For those who experience multiple marriages and deaths, Social Security provides flexibility while preventing double benefits. By the same token, if you're, sadly, twice widowed, you can't collect survivor benefits on the earnings records of both late spouses. You'll get whichever one is higher — unless your own retirement benefit is bigger still, in which case you'll get that.

Medicare eligibility generally isn't affected by remarriage, as it's an individual program based on age and work history rather than family status. However, if you're receiving Medicare based on a deceased spouse's work record and you remarry someone who also has Medicare eligibility, you may want to compare the costs and benefits of each option.

Supplemental Security Income (SSI) faces different rules regarding remarriage, as it's a needs-based program that considers household income and resources. Supplemental Security Income (SSI) payments – Your SSI eligibility and payment amount may change (or stop) due to your new spouse's income and resources. If you and your spouse both get SSI, your payment amount may change from a single person's rate to a couple's rate.

The timing of reporting your remarriage to Social Security is crucial to avoid overpayments and potential penalties. Be sure to call us right away at 1-800-772-1213 to report your marriage to avoid being overpaid. Overpayments can result in significant financial hardship if Social Security later demands repayment of benefits you weren't entitled to receive.

COBRA Rights for Surviving Spouses

When an employee dies, their surviving family members face not only emotional trauma but also the immediate loss of employer-provided health insurance. COBRA (Consolidated Omnibus Budget Reconciliation Act) provides crucial protection during this vulnerable time, allowing surviving spouses and dependent children to maintain their health coverage while transitioning to alternative insurance options.

COBRA coverage for surviving spouses lasts significantly longer than the typical 18-month period available to employees who lose their jobs. If the qualifying event is the death of the covered employee, divorce or legal separation of the covered employee from the covered employee's spouse, or the covered employee becoming entitled to Medicare, COBRA for the spouse or dependent child lasts for 36 months.

This extended 36-month period recognizes that death creates a permanent loss of coverage opportunity, unlike temporary unemployment where the individual might find new employer coverage. The three-year window provides surviving spouses with substantial time to secure alternative health insurance, whether through new employment, Medicare eligibility, or individual market plans.

Understanding who qualifies as a "qualified beneficiary" under COBRA is essential for surviving family members. A qualified beneficiary is an individual who is entitled to COBRA continuation coverage because he or she was covered by a group health plan on the day before a "qualifying event." Depending on the circumstances, the following individuals may be qualified beneficiaries: a "covered employee" (a term that includes active employees, terminated employees and retirees); a covered employee's spouse and dependent children.

The notification process following a death involves specific responsibilities for both employers and family members. Plan administrators must notify qualified beneficiaries of their right to elect COBRA coverage once they receive notice of the qualifying event. Each qualified beneficiary then has 60 days to decide whether to elect continuation coverage. This 60-day election period is crucial, as missing this deadline means losing the right to COBRA coverage entirely.

COBRA coverage typically requires paying the full premium cost plus an administrative fee. Generally, your coverage under COBRA will be the same coverage you had while you were an employee. This is helpful if you would like to continue to see your same doctors and receive the same health plan benefits. Your dependents (i.e., spouse, former spouse or children) are also eligible for COBRA coverage, even if you (the former employee) do not sign up for COBRA coverage.

The cost of COBRA coverage can be substantial, often representing the first time families see the true cost of their health insurance. Qualified individuals may be required to pay the entire premium for coverage up to 102% of the cost to the plan. For many surviving spouses, this cost may be prohibitive, making it essential to explore alternative coverage options.

Each qualified beneficiary has independent election rights, meaning surviving spouses and dependent children can make separate decisions about COBRA coverage. Perhaps most importantly, each qualified beneficiary has a separate right to elect COBRA continuation coverage. For example, the employee's spouse may elect continuation coverage even if the employee does not. COBRA continuation coverage may be elected for only one, several, or all dependent children who are qualified beneficiaries.

In certain circumstances, disability can extend COBRA coverage beyond the standard 36-month period. If you or any of your dependents are certified as disabled (Title II or XVI), you may continue COBRA coverage for up to an additional 11 months. This provision provides crucial protection for families dealing with both the death of a loved one and disability challenges.

For surviving spouses who become eligible for Medicare during their COBRA period, important coordination rules apply. If you continue coverage under COBRA before you are eligible for Medicare, you must enroll in Medicare when you are first eligible. Your COBRA coverage ends when you are eligible for Medicare, even if you are still within your initial COBRA eligibility period.

The relationship between COBRA and special enrollment rights in other plans provides additional flexibility for surviving families. If you decide to elect COBRA coverage under your plan, special enrollment also is available in a spouse's plan after COBRA continuation coverage is exhausted. This coordination ensures that families don't face gaps in coverage when COBRA ends.

Special Enrollment Rights After Life Events

Major life events like death, divorce, and other qualifying changes trigger special enrollment periods (SEPs) that allow individuals to make health insurance changes outside of standard enrollment windows. These protections are crucial for maintaining continuous coverage during life's most challenging transitions, preventing gaps that could prove financially devastating.

Medicare Special Enrollment Periods provide flexibility for those experiencing major life changes while enrolled in Medicare. You can make changes to your Medicare Advantage and Medicare drug coverage when certain events happen in your life, like if you move or you lose other coverage. These chances to make changes are called Special Enrollment Periods.

Death of a spouse constitutes a qualifying event for several types of special enrollment periods. For those with marketplace health insurance, You'll qualify for a Special Enrollment Period if someone on your Marketplace plan dies which causes you to lose your current health plan. This protection ensures that surviving spouses don't lose health coverage during an already difficult time.

Divorce creates additional special enrollment opportunities, though the specific circumstances matter. You may qualify for a Special Enrollment Period if you lose qualifying health coverage you had through a parent, spouse, or other family member. This might happen if you lose health coverage because: Of a divorce or legal separation. However, Divorce or legal separation without losing coverage doesn't qualify you for a Special Enrollment Period.

The timing of special enrollment periods is critical, with most lasting only 60 days from the qualifying event. Most SEPs last 60 days and require documentation to prove eligibility. Missing these deadlines can result in waiting until the next open enrollment period, potentially leaving individuals without coverage for months.

For Medicare beneficiaries, household changes that affect coverage can trigger special enrollment rights. Some SEPs are triggered by life events that affect your household structure, which may in turn impact your access to healthcare coverage. Marriage or Divorce: Especially if the event affects your access to health coverage. Death of a Spouse: If you lose spousal coverage.

Loss of employer coverage, including through COBRA exhaustion, creates special enrollment opportunities in multiple programs. End of COBRA or Creditable Drug Coverage: Loss of employer-based coverage or COBRA can trigger an 8-month Special Enrollment Period for Part B. However, the Part D enrollment window is shorter—typically 63 days from the loss of creditable drug coverage.

For those with both Medicare and employer coverage, the coordination rules create specific enrollment opportunities. If you're eligible for Medicare but still working, special enrollment periods protect you from penalties when your employment situation changes. If you or your spouse have health insurance through your job, you can sign up: Any time while working and still covered by the group health plan. Within 8 months of the day you or your spouse stop working, even if your group health plan continues for a time.

Documentation requirements for special enrollment periods vary by program and qualifying event, but generally require proof of the life change that triggered eligibility. When you experience a qualifying life event, you may be asked for documents to confirm the life event. The type of documentation you need depends on the type of qualifying life event.

Missing special enrollment deadlines can have serious consequences, including late enrollment penalties that last for years. Avoid the penalty & gap in coverage If you miss this 8-month Special Enrollment Period , you'll have to wait to sign up and go months without coverage. You might also pay a monthly penalty for as long as you have Part B. The penalty goes up the longer you wait to sign up.

The complexity of coordinating multiple programs during major life events makes professional guidance valuable for many individuals. Understanding which special enrollment periods apply to your specific situation, gathering required documentation, and meeting critical deadlines can determine whether you maintain continuous coverage or face costly gaps and penalties.

Major life events test both our emotional resilience and our understanding of complex benefit systems. By knowing your rights and options before you need them, you can navigate these challenging transitions with confidence, protecting both your health and your financial security during life's most difficult moments.

CHAPTER 12: GEOGRAPHIC CONSIDERATIONS - MOVING IN RETIREMENT

When Robert and Linda started planning their retirement five years ago, they had a simple dream: selling their home in expensive Connecticut and moving to a warm, affordable state where their pension and Social Security would stretch further. What began as casual conversations about "someday" quickly evolved into serious research when they realized that their choice of retirement destination could save them thousands of dollars annually—or cost them dearly if they chose wrong. From Linda's discovery that Connecticut taxes Social Security benefits while neighboring states don't, to Robert's realization that his Medicare Advantage plan wouldn't work in Florida, their retirement planning suddenly became a complex geographic puzzle with significant financial implications.

The decision of where to spend your retirement years has never been more important. Beyond considerations of climate, cost of living, and proximity to family, retirees must now navigate a maze of state-specific rules governing Medicare plan availability, Social Security taxation, and healthcare coverage that can dramatically impact their financial security. The difference between choosing wisely and choosing poorly can amount to tens of thousands of dollars over the course of retirement. This chapter will guide you through the critical geographic considerations that affect your Medicare and Social Security benefits, helping you make informed decisions about where to call home in your golden years—whether that's across town, across the country, or even across the world.

Medicare Plan Availability by State

One of the most surprising discoveries many retirees make is that Medicare isn't truly "national" when it comes to plan options. While Original Medicare (Parts A and B) provides the same basic coverage everywhere in the United States, Medicare Advantage plans and prescription drug plans vary dramatically by location, creating significant disparities in available options, costs, and benefits.

The average Medicare beneficiary will have the option of 34 Medicare Advantage prescription drug (MA-PD) plans in 2025, 2 fewer than the 36 options available in 2024. However, this national average masks substantial regional variations that can affect your healthcare choices and costs. The number of plans available to the average beneficiary varies across states. In 27 states and Puerto Rico, the average beneficiary has a choice of fewer plans in 2025 than in 2024, while in 16 states and DC, the average beneficiary has a choice of more plans.

The geographic lottery of Medicare plan availability becomes even more pronounced when examining the extremes. Nearly one-third of Medicare beneficiaries (32%) live in a county with more than 50 Medicare Advantage plans available in 2025, up from 7 percent in 2020, and similar to 2024 (33%). Less than 0.5

percent live in a county with no plans available. This means that depending on where you live, you might choose from dozens of plans with competitive pricing and robust benefits, or you might face limited options with higher costs.

The variation in plan availability directly impacts not just choice, but also quality and cost. In 2025, there are standard 5-star Medicare Advantage plans in 13 states and Puerto Rico. If you don't live in one of these states, you may not have access to the highest-rated plans available, potentially affecting the quality of care and member satisfaction you experience.

Special Needs Plans (SNPs) represent another area where geography matters significantly. More Special Needs Plans (SNPs) will be available. Medicare Advantage plans can offer SNPs to people with Medicare with specific health conditions, certain health care needs, or who also have Medicaid. The number of SNP offerings will grow by 9% between 2024 and 2025 and represents about a quarter of total plans. However, these specialized plans aren't available everywhere, meaning that beneficiaries with chronic conditions or dual eligibility for Medicare and Medicaid may find better options in some states than others.

The prescription drug landscape also varies significantly by geography. A total of 464 PDPs will be offered by these 7 firms in the 34 PDP regions (plus another 10 PDPs in the territories), a decrease of 245 PDPs (-35%) from 2024, and the lowest number of PDPs available in any year since Part D started in 2006. Despite the reduction in PDP availability overall, beneficiaries in each state will have a choice of multiple plans, ranging from 12 PDPs in 12 states to 21 PDPs in other areas.

Premium costs for identical coverage can vary substantially across different markets due to local competition, provider networks, and healthcare costs. Among the 12 national PDPs, there is a difference of more than $1,500 in average annual premiums between the highest-premium PDP and the lowest-premium PDP. While this represents the national range, regional variations can also be significant, making location a crucial factor in prescription drug costs.

Understanding these geographic disparities is essential for retirement planning. If you're considering relocating, researching Medicare plan availability in your target destination should be as important as investigating housing costs or state tax policies. The Medicare Plan Finder at Medicare.gov allows you to compare plans by ZIP code, providing insight into what options would be available in different locations.

Moving and Your Medicare Coverage

When you relocate during retirement, your Medicare coverage doesn't simply transfer unchanged to your new location. Understanding the rules and opportunities that come with moving can help you optimize your coverage and avoid costly mistakes or coverage gaps.

Moving triggers one of Medicare's most important Special Enrollment Periods (SEPs), providing flexibility that many beneficiaries don't realize they have. You can make changes to your Medicare Advantage and Medicare drug coverage when certain events happen in your life, like if you move or you lose other coverage. These chances to make changes are called Special Enrollment Periods.

The timing of when you notify your plan about your move affects the length of your enrollment window. Your chance to switch begins when you move and continues for 2 full months after you move. If you tell your plan before you move, your chance to switch plans begins the month before the month you move and continues for 2 full months after you move. This advance notification can be particularly valuable if you want your new coverage to start immediately upon arrival in your new state.

The type of move determines what coverage changes you can make. For moves that take you outside your current plan's service area, you have broad flexibility. You can also choose to go back to Original Medicare if you're in a Medicare Advantage Plan and you move outside your plan's service area. If you move outside your old plan's service area and don't join a new Medicare Advantage Plan during this Special Enrollment Period, you'll be enrolled in Original Medicare when you're dropped from your old Medicare Advantage Plan.

Even moves within your plan's service area can create opportunities if new plan options become available in your new location. I moved to a new address that's still in my plan's service area, but I have new plan options in my new location... Switch to a new Medicare Advantage Plan (with or without drug coverage) or Medicare drug plan. This provision recognizes that even local moves can change your access to providers or create opportunities for better coverage.

For those returning to the United States after living abroad, special rules apply. I moved back to the U.S after living outside the country... Join a Medicare Advantage Plan or Medicare drug plan... Your chance to join lasts for 2 full months after the month you move back to the U.S. This SEP can be crucial for expats who maintained their Medicare coverage while living overseas.

Planning your move strategically can help optimize your Medicare coverage. If you're considering relocating, research the Medicare plans available in your target destination before you move. Use the

Medicare Plan Finder to compare options, and consider timing your move to align with enrollment periods for maximum flexibility.

Important considerations for your move include ensuring continuity of care with specialists or ongoing treatments, understanding how your prescription drug coverage might change, and evaluating whether your current providers have locations or affiliates in your new area. If you have chronic conditions requiring ongoing care, investigating the provider networks in your new location should be a priority in your relocation planning.

State-Specific Medicare Supplement Rules

While Medicare Advantage plans vary significantly by location, Medicare Supplement (Medigap) policies might seem more standardized—but state-specific rules create important variations that can significantly impact your coverage options and costs, particularly if you're under 65 or have special circumstances.

The federal government standardizes most Medigap policies, but important exceptions exist. All Medigap policies are standardized. This means, policies with the same letter offer the same basic benefits no matter where you live or which insurance company you buy the policy from. There are 10 different types of Medigap plans offered in most states, which are named by letters: A-D, F, G, and K-N. However, Important: In Massachusetts, Minnesota, and Wisconsin, Medigap policies are standardized in a different way.

These three states have their own standardization systems that predate federal requirements. If you're moving to or from Massachusetts, Minnesota, or Wisconsin, you'll need to understand how their unique Medigap systems work and how they might affect your coverage options.

For beneficiaries under 65 who qualify for Medicare due to disability, state rules vary dramatically. Federal law doesn't require companies to sell Medigap policies to people under 65. This creates a patchwork of state regulations that can significantly impact disabled beneficiaries' access to supplemental coverage.

Some states provide no guaranteed access to Medigap for under-65 beneficiaries. These states have not enacted any provisions to ensure access to supplemental coverage for Medicare beneficiaries who are under age 65, and there do not appear to be any guaranteed-issue plans available for this population: Nevada... Ohio. Legislation is under consideration in both states to improve access.

Other states require insurers to offer some, but not all, Medigap plans to under-65 beneficiaries. In these states, insurers are required to offer some – but not all – of their Medigap plans to people under 65. State regulations vary in terms of the specific plans that have to be offered and whether the insurer can charge higher premiums for under-65 enrollees. For example, North Carolina G.S. 58-54-45 guarantees that individuals under the age of 65 who qualify for Medicare are eligible to purchase a Medigap policy A, D, or G effective January 1, 2020.

Some states maintain high-risk pools to provide coverage options for under-65 beneficiaries. Some of these high-risk pools are currently only open to Medicare beneficiaries who need supplemental coverage, although some continue to also offer coverage for people who don't have other individual market (non-Medicare) coverage. However, some states are phasing out these options.

The timing of Medigap enrollment is crucial regardless of your state. You get a 6 month "Medigap Open Enrollment" period, which starts the first month you have Medicare Part B and you're 65 or older. During this time, you can enroll in any Medigap policy and the insurance company can't deny you coverage due to pre-existing health problems. After this period, you may not be able to buy a Medigap policy, or it may cost more.

If you're planning to move during or after your Medigap Open Enrollment Period, timing becomes critical. When your employer coverage ends, you'll have a chance to sign up for Part B without paying a Late Enrollment Penalty. Your one-time Medigap Open Enrollment Period starts once you sign up for Part B and lasts for 6 months, even if you sign up for Part B while you still have employer coverage.

Moving generally doesn't create new Medigap enrollment rights, so planning ahead is essential. If you're considering relocating and want Medigap coverage, it's typically better to obtain it before moving rather than hoping to qualify for coverage in your new state under potentially more restrictive rules.

Social Security and State Taxes

One of the most impactful financial considerations when choosing a retirement destination is how different states treat Social Security benefits for tax purposes. The landscape has been rapidly changing in favor of retirees, but significant differences remain that can affect your after-tax retirement income.

The trend has been overwhelmingly positive for retirees in recent years. Nine states still tax Social Security benefits in 2025, but that number could continue to shrink, with West Virginia phasing out its tax and lawmakers in other states trying to do the same. This represents a dramatic shift from historical patterns, with Most states, 41 in total plus Washington, D.C., won't tax your Social Security benefits in 2025, based on current laws.

Recent changes have provided significant relief for retirees. Missouri and Nebraska have decided to stop taxing Social Security benefits in 2024. Kansas also joined in with a bill signed midway through 2024, so the state will not tax Social Security going forward. These changes can represent substantial savings for affected retirees.

The nine states that continue to tax Social Security benefits in 2025 are: Colorado, Connecticut, Minnesota, Montana, New Mexico, Rhode Island, Utah, Vermont and West Virginia. However, each of these states has its own rules and exemptions that may protect many retirees from taxation.

Colorado offers significant protections for most retirees. Colorado taxpayers who are 65 and older as of Dec. 31 of the tax year can subtract the full amount of their Social Security benefits from their Colorado tax return. Taxpayers aged 55-64 can deduct all Social Security benefits if their adjusted gross income is $75,000 or less (individual) or $95,000 or less (couple filing jointly).

Connecticut provides income-based exemptions. Connecticut taxpayers whose adjusted gross income is $75,000 or less (individuals and married filing separately) or $100,000 or less (joint filers and heads of household) can deduct 100 percent of their federally taxable Social Security income.

Minnesota has complex but generous rules for many retirees. Minnesota taxes Social Security income that is considered taxable by the federal government, but Minnesota allows taxpayers to subtract a portion of their Social Security payments from their adjusted income as long as they meet certain income thresholds. In 2025, the simplified method allows taxpayers with AGIs below $108,320 for married joint returns — or $84,490 for single or head of household filers — to subtract all taxable Social Security benefits.

West Virginia is in the process of eliminating its Social Security tax entirely. West Virginia has long taxed Social Security benefits, and it still does as of 2024 and 2025. However, the state has begun a three-year phase-out program to eliminate these taxes by 2026. More specifically, taxpayers of all income levels will be able to exempt 35% of Social Security income on their 2024 taxes, 65% on their 2025 taxes and 100% on their 2026 taxes.

The financial impact of these state tax differences can be substantial. The savings from living in a state that doesn't tax Social Security benefits depends on your total benefit amount and the state's tax rate. "So, for example, if your effective rate in your state was 5%, and you received $30,000 in Social Security benefits, that would be a savings of $1,500," Kuhn said.

The collective impact across entire states demonstrates the significance of these policies. "In Missouri, for instance, retirees are looking at a collective annual saving of around $309 million," said Jeff Rose, CFP, founder of Good Financial Cents. "Over in Nebraska, it's about $17 million. That's a lot of money that retirees get to keep in their pockets instead of it being drained away by state taxes".

When evaluating potential retirement destinations, Social Security tax treatment should be weighed alongside other factors like overall tax burden, cost of living, and quality of life. A state that doesn't tax Social Security benefits might have higher property taxes or sales taxes that offset some of the savings.

International Considerations for Expats

For the growing number of Americans choosing to spend their retirement years abroad, understanding how Medicare and Social Security work internationally is crucial for maintaining benefits and avoiding costly mistakes. The rules are complex and often misunderstood, making careful planning essential.

Medicare coverage outside the United States is extremely limited. Medicare does not cover medical services or health care administered abroad. But it will cover beneficiaries who live abroad when they travel to the U.S. and in certain emergency situations outside the U.S. This fundamental limitation means that retirees living abroad must secure alternative health insurance for their daily healthcare needs.

Despite limited coverage abroad, maintaining Medicare enrollment can still be worthwhile for some expats. You can have Medicare while you live abroad, but it will usually not cover the care you receive. Most people qualify for premium-free Part A, meaning you will pay nothing for coverage. Keeping Part A costs nothing for most beneficiaries and maintains eligibility for Medicare coverage when visiting the United States.

Part B decisions are more complex for expats due to the monthly premium requirement. "Medicare Part B comes with a monthly premium that is typically taken from your Social Security payment," Stidom says. In 2025, the base premium for Part B is $185 per month. Whether this cost is worthwhile depends on how frequently you return to the United States and your long-term plans.

The decision to maintain or drop Part B has long-term consequences. "If you choose not to enroll in Part B while living abroad, you will need to provide documentation proving you were living outside of the

U.S. in order to enroll upon your return and avoid a penalty for delaying enrollment in Part B," Stidom adds. This documentation requirement makes record-keeping crucial for expats.

Enrollment opportunities exist for returning expats, but timing matters. If you were living outside the U.S. when you turned 65 and don't qualify for Social Security benefits, then upon returning to the United States as a permanent resident, your special enrollment period will begin (lasting for three months). Your coverage begins on the first day of the month after you enroll.

Medicare Advantage and Part D plans generally cannot be maintained while living abroad. If you have a Medicare Advantage or Medicare Part D plan before you move abroad, you should disenroll and stop paying these premiums when you move because these plans require that you live in their service area in order to be enrolled.

Social Security benefits can generally continue while living abroad, but with restrictions. If you get Social Security benefits, you can still receive payments while you visit or live in most foreign countries. However, Generally, we cannot pay Retirement, Survivors, and Disability Insurance benefits to noncitizens after their sixth calendar month outside the United States. However, you might qualify for an exception, which could allow you to receive benefits without visiting the United States.

For U.S. citizens, Social Security payments can continue abroad with fewer restrictions. If you are a U.S. citizen, you may receive your Social Security payments outside the U.S. as long as you are eligible for them. However, there are certain countries to which we are not allowed to send payments.

Social Security maintains oversight of overseas beneficiaries through periodic questionnaires. Once you begin receiving Social Security benefits abroad, SSA will send you a questionnaire every 1 to 2 years. This questionnaire will determine if you are still eligible for benefits. If you do not respond, SSA may stop your benefit payments.

Special considerations apply to expats who volunteer internationally. You volunteer internationally for at least 12 months for a tax-exempt non-profit organization and have health insurance during that time. You will have a six-month Special Enrollment Period to enroll in Medicare without gaps or penalties.

For expats planning to return to the United States, maintaining some Medicare coverage can prevent gaps and penalties. For those planning permanent residence abroad, the costs of maintaining U.S. Medicare coverage may not be justified, making local health insurance or international health insurance more practical options.

Understanding these international rules before relocating abroad is essential for making informed decisions about benefit maintenance, healthcare coverage, and long-term financial planning. Consulting with the Social Security Administration and Medicare before making the move can help prevent costly mistakes and ensure continued access to benefits you've earned.

CHAPTER 13: RETIREMENT INCOME PLANNING

Retirement income planning represents one of the most critical yet complex aspects of your financial journey. Unlike the accumulation phase where you focused on building wealth, retirement requires a fundamental shift toward strategically distributing your assets to create sustainable income streams that will last throughout your golden years. This transition demands careful orchestration of multiple income sources, thoughtful tax planning, and proactive management of healthcare costs and estate considerations.

The landscape of retirement income planning has evolved significantly in recent years. According to J.P. Morgan research, six in 10 retirees experience spending fluctuations of 20% for each of the first three years of their retirement, and half of retirees between ages 75 and 80 continue to experience this spending volatility from year to year. This reality underscores the importance of developing flexible strategies that can adapt to changing circumstances while maintaining financial security. Understanding how to coordinate Social Security benefits with other retirement income sources, implement tax-efficient withdrawal strategies, plan for healthcare costs, and protect your legacy through proper estate planning will determine whether your retirement years are characterized by financial confidence or constant worry.

Coordinating Social Security with Other Retirement Income

Social Security benefits form the foundation of most Americans' retirement income, but maximizing their value requires strategic coordination with your other income sources. Research indicates that waiting until age 70 to claim Social Security can boost benefit checks by 24% compared to claiming at full retirement age for those born in 1960 or later. However, this decision cannot be made in isolation—it must be evaluated within the context of your overall retirement income strategy.

The timing of Social Security claims significantly impacts your tax situation and withdrawal strategies from other accounts. Before Social Security begins, retirees have more flexibility in the strategies they choose to draw down their accounts. This creates a unique opportunity during early retirement years to implement tax-smoothing strategies, such as Roth conversions or controlled withdrawals from tax-deferred accounts to fill lower tax brackets.

When coordinating Social Security with other income sources, consider the taxation implications carefully. Up to 85% of your Social Security benefits may be subject to federal income tax depending on your combined income, which includes your adjusted gross income, nontaxable interest, and half of your Social Security benefits. This creates what's known as the "tax torpedo"—a situation where additional income can cause a disproportionate increase in taxes by triggering taxation of previously untaxed Social Security benefits.

For couples, spousal benefits and survivor benefits add another layer of complexity to coordination strategies. The higher-earning spouse's decision to delay claiming can significantly increase survivor benefits, providing crucial protection for the longer-lived spouse. Research shows that having more guaranteed income may result in increased spending in retirement, for households with similar levels of total retirement wealth, because people feel comfortable spending Social Security pensions and annuities while they are more reluctant to spend the capital of their portfolio.

Tax-Efficient Withdrawal Strategies

Creating a tax-efficient withdrawal strategy is essential for maximizing the longevity of your retirement savings. One study showed that strategically drawing down investment accounts in a tax-efficient order extended a hypothetical portfolio's longevity by more than two and a half years. The key lies in understanding the tax characteristics of your various account types and implementing a strategic sequence that minimizes your overall tax burden.

The traditional approach suggests withdrawing from accounts in this order: taxable accounts first, then tax-deferred accounts (traditional IRAs and 401(k)s), and finally tax-free accounts (Roth IRAs). This strategy allows tax-advantaged accounts to continue growing on a tax-deferred basis, while taxable accounts are subject to ongoing taxation. However, this conventional wisdom requires modification based on your specific circumstances.

The proportional approach can be more effective than the traditional sequential method. By spreading out taxable income more evenly over retirement, you may be able to reduce the taxes you pay on Social Security benefits and the premiums you pay on Medicare. This strategy involves taking distributions from multiple account types simultaneously in proportions designed to optimize your tax situation year by year.

Several factors can justify deviating from standard withdrawal sequences. If retirees have low taxable income and are in a lower tax bracket, it might make sense to draw from a 401(k) or traditional IRA to take advantage of lower rates before Required Minimum Distributions begin. This is particularly relevant for early retirees who have several years before Social Security and RMDs begin.

Roth conversions represent another powerful tool in tax-efficient withdrawal planning. Roth conversions are an ideal way to fill up low tax brackets in early retirement while keeping as much money as possible in tax-advantaged accounts. However, at lower income levels, the potential benefit of a conversion at a low tax rate is largely negated by higher taxation of Social Security benefits.

Tax-loss harvesting in taxable accounts can further enhance efficiency. This involves selling investments that have decreased in value to realize a loss, which can then be used to counterbalance gains from other investments. Additionally, up to $3,000 of net capital losses can be used to offset other types of income each year.

Healthcare Costs in Retirement Planning

Healthcare expenses represent one of the largest and least predictable costs in retirement, making them a critical component of income planning. A 65-year-old retiring in 2025 can expect to spend an average of $172,500 in health care and medical expenses throughout retirement, representing a more than 4% increase over 2024. This figure assumes enrollment in Medicare Parts A, B, and D, yet still leaves significant out-of-pocket expenses.

The challenge with healthcare cost planning extends beyond the dollar amounts. A healthy 65-year-old couple can expect to spend upwards of $395,000 on healthcare costs in retirement, with costs varying significantly based on when a person retires, where they live, and which coverage they choose. These variations make personalized planning essential rather than relying on general estimates.

Medicare provides the foundation of healthcare coverage for most retirees, but understanding its limitations is crucial for proper planning. While 37% of Americans plan to rely on Medicare to cover health care costs in retirement, Fidelity's estimate shows how quickly out-of-pocket expenses can add up. Retirees are still on the hook to cover things like Medicare premiums, over-the-counter medications, dental and vision care, and other types of added expenses like long-term care.

Timing of retirement significantly impacts healthcare costs. If a person retires five years earlier, at age 60, they can expect to pay 56% more for healthcare expenses than if they wait until age 65 and enroll in Original Medicare plus Medigap, or 89% more than if they wait until age 65 and enroll in an MAPD plan. This cost differential makes healthcare considerations a crucial factor in retirement timing decisions.

Health Savings Accounts (HSAs) offer the most tax-efficient way to save for healthcare expenses. An HSA can help you save tax-efficiently for health care costs in retirement. You can save pretax dollars which have the potential to grow and be withdrawn tax-free for federal and state tax purposes if used for qualified medical expenses. For 2025, you can make tax-deductible contributions of up to $4,300 for individual coverage and $8,550 for family coverage, plus an additional $1,000 for those ages 55 and older.

Long-term care represents a particularly significant risk that requires separate planning consideration. Long-term care insurance can seem costly—annual premiums with 3% growth for a healthy 60-year-old average $2,585 for males and $4,400 for females—but with the median annual cost of a private room in a nursing home at $116,800, it may be more expensive not to have it.

Impact of Asset Sales on Medicare Premiums

One of the most overlooked aspects of retirement income planning is how asset sales and other income events can trigger higher Medicare premiums through the Income-Related Monthly Adjustment Amount (IRMAA). IRMAA is a surcharge that people with income above a certain amount must pay in addition to their Medicare Part B and Part D premiums, based on income reported two years prior.

For 2025, Medicare beneficiaries with income above $106,000 for single tax filers, $212,000 for joint filers, and $106,000 for married people who file separately will pay the surcharge, with total Monthly Part B premiums ranging from $259 to $628.90. The structure creates what's known as a "cliff" effect, where if your income crosses over to the next bracket by $1, all of a sudden, your Medicare premiums can jump by over $1,000 per year.

Understanding IRMAA's timing is crucial for retirement planning. The income on your 2023 IRS tax return determines the IRMAA you pay in 2025. This two-year lag creates both challenges and opportunities for strategic planning. Large asset sales, such as selling real estate or business interests, can trigger IRMAA charges even if your ongoing retirement income is modest.

The types of income that contribute to IRMAA calculations include typical retirement income sources. Income used to determine the IRMAA comes from sources typically used by many retirees, including taxable distributions from traditional IRAs, 401(k)s, 403(b)s, and Social Security benefits. This makes IRMAA planning an integral part of withdrawal strategy development.

Strategic planning can help minimize IRMAA impact. To avoid this risk, be sure to properly time a Roth conversion; you can then avoid the IRMAA when you take tax-free distributions. Additionally, taking steps to reduce your MAGI could lower your medical costs. You can take a qualified charitable distribution to help reduce your MAGI, donating up to $108,000 in 2025 to a qualified charity directly from your retirement account.

For retirees with significant unrealized gains, the step-up in basis at death provides important estate planning considerations. If they don't need to sell those assets during their lifetime, their heirs will receive a step-up in basis upon inheritance, effectively eliminating capital gains taxes on past appreciation.

Estate Planning Considerations

Estate planning in retirement requires coordination with income planning to ensure both current financial security and efficient wealth transfer. Retirees should have five essential estate planning documents in place: a last will, a durable power of attorney, an advance healthcare directive, a HIPAA release form, and, if significant assets or property are involved, a revocable living trust.

The current estate planning environment presents unique opportunities and challenges. The federal estate and gift tax exemption amounts are $13.99 million in 2025, but absent any changes in the law, the increased exemptions under the TCJA are set to 'sunset' as of January 1, 2026, back to approximately $7 million. This creates urgency for high-net-worth individuals to implement wealth transfer strategies.

Beneficiary designations on retirement accounts require special attention because they supersede will provisions. These designations take legal precedence over a will, so failing to revise them after major life changes can lead to assets being distributed in ways that don't reflect the retiree's true wishes. The SECURE Act has significantly impacted inherited retirement account planning, generally requiring non-spouse beneficiaries to withdraw inherited account balances within ten years.

For taxpayers who live in states with a state estate tax but no state gift tax, lifetime gifting will have the effect of reducing the state estate tax liability. This creates additional planning opportunities for residents of certain states to optimize their overall tax situation.

Revocable living trusts offer particular advantages for retirees. Unlike a will, which only takes effect after death, a living trust operates immediately and continues seamlessly through incapacity and death. This continuity can be especially valuable for managing complex retirement income streams and investment portfolios.

Long-term care planning intersects significantly with estate planning. Retirees can strengthen their estate plan by making sure it includes a long-term care strategy, which may involve purchasing long-term care insurance or establishing an asset protection trust.

The integration of estate planning with retirement income planning requires ongoing attention to tax efficiency. Roth assets avoid required minimum distributions during the employee and their surviving spouse's lifetime, making them powerful from both a compounding and future income tax management perspective, as well as an attractive asset to inherit.

Conclusion

Successful retirement income planning requires a holistic approach that coordinates multiple income sources, implements tax-efficient strategies, plans for healthcare costs, manages Medicare premium impacts, and preserves wealth for future generations. The complexity of these interconnected decisions underscores the importance of developing a comprehensive strategy early in retirement and adjusting it as circumstances change.

The key to long-term success lies in understanding that retirement income planning is not a one-time event but an ongoing process requiring regular review and adjustment. Market conditions, tax laws, healthcare costs, and personal circumstances will all evolve throughout retirement, necessitating flexibility and adaptability in your approach.

By implementing the strategies outlined in this chapter—coordinating Social Security optimally, employing tax-efficient withdrawal sequences, planning proactively for healthcare costs, managing IRMAA exposure, and integrating estate planning considerations—you can create a robust framework for financial security throughout your retirement years. Remember that professional guidance can be invaluable in navigating these complex decisions and ensuring your retirement income plan aligns with your unique circumstances and goals.

CHAPTER 14: MANAGING HEALTHCARE COSTS IN RETIREMENT

Healthcare costs represent one of the most significant and unpredictable expenses retirees will face, yet they remain among the most overlooked aspects of retirement planning. The sobering reality is that a 65-year-old retiring in 2025 can expect to spend an average of $172,500 in healthcare and medical expenses throughout retirement—a figure that represents a more than 4% increase over 2024 and continues an upward trajectory that has seen costs more than double since Fidelity began tracking these expenses in 2002.

Understanding how to effectively manage these costs is not just about preserving your financial security; it's about maintaining your quality of life and independence throughout your golden years. Healthcare expenses in retirement extend far beyond what Medicare covers, encompassing everything from prescription medications and dental care to long-term care services that can easily cost six figures annually. The challenge is compounded by the fact that healthcare inflation consistently outpaces general inflation, making accurate planning even more critical. This chapter will equip you with the knowledge and strategies needed to budget effectively for Medicare premiums and out-of-pocket costs, maximize the benefits of Health Savings Accounts, navigate supplemental insurance options, address gaps in dental, vision, and hearing coverage, and manage the escalating costs associated with chronic conditions that become increasingly common with age.

Budgeting for Medicare Premiums and Out-of-Pocket Costs

Medicare forms the foundation of healthcare coverage for most retirees, but understanding its true costs is essential for accurate retirement budgeting. The standard monthly premium for Medicare Part B will be $185.00 in 2025, an increase of $10.30 from $174.70 in 2024. However, this base premium represents just the beginning of your Medicare-related expenses.

The annual deductible for all Medicare Part B beneficiaries will be $257 in 2025, an increase of $17 from the 2024 deductible of $240. After meeting this deductible, you'll typically pay 20% coinsurance for most outpatient services, with no annual limit on your out-of-pocket costs unless you have supplemental coverage. This lack of an out-of-pocket maximum in Original Medicare represents one of its most significant limitations.

Medicare Part A, while premium-free for most beneficiaries who have worked and paid Medicare taxes for at least 40 quarters, carries substantial cost-sharing requirements. The Part A inpatient hospital deductible will increase to $1,676 in 2025, up $44 from 2024. If you require extended hospital stays, coinsurance kicks in at $419 per day for days 61-90 of hospitalization in a benefit period, and $838 per day for lifetime reserve days.

For prescription drug coverage under Medicare Part D, premiums vary by plan but average around $46.50 per month in 2025. Importantly, beginning in 2025, all Part D plans will have a $2,000 annual cap on out-of-pocket prescription drug costs, down from the previous $8,000 cap. This represents significant savings for those with high prescription drug costs.

Higher-income beneficiaries face additional costs through the Income-Related Monthly Adjustment Amount (IRMAA). If your 2023 modified adjusted gross income exceeded $106,000 as an individual or $212,000 for married couples filing jointly, you'll pay additional premiums ranging from $74 to $443.90 monthly for Part B, and from $13.70 to $85.80 monthly for Part D.

When budgeting for Medicare costs, consider these practical strategies. First, understand that Medicare premiums are typically deducted from Social Security benefits, potentially reducing your monthly cash flow. Plan for this reduction when calculating your retirement income needs. Second, factor in regional cost variations, as healthcare costs can vary significantly by geographic location. Third, remember that Medicare doesn't cover everything—notably excluding most dental, vision, and hearing care, as well as long-term care services.

Creating an accurate healthcare budget requires projecting both fixed costs (premiums and deductibles) and variable costs (coinsurance and services not covered by Medicare). Financial advisors recommend allocating 15% of your total retirement budget to healthcare expenses, though this percentage may need to increase for those with chronic conditions or those who retire before age 65 when Medicare begins.

Health Savings Accounts as Retirement Tools

Health Savings Accounts represent one of the most powerful yet underutilized tools for retirement healthcare planning, offering what many consider the ultimate "triple tax advantage." HSAs allow tax-deductible contributions, tax-free growth, and tax-free withdrawals for qualified medical expenses, making them exceptionally valuable for retirement planning.

For 2025, HSA contribution limits have increased to $4,300 for self-only coverage and $8,550 for family coverage. Individuals age 55 and older can contribute an additional $1,000 as a catch-up contribution, allowing them to save up to $5,300 individually or $9,550 per family. These contribution limits continue to rise annually with inflation, providing increased opportunities to save for healthcare costs.

To contribute to an HSA, you must be enrolled in a high-deductible health plan (HDHP). For 2025, this means having a plan with an annual deductible of at least $1,650 for self-only coverage or $3,300 for family coverage, and out-of-pocket maximums that don't exceed $8,300 for individual plans or $16,600 for family coverage.

The strategic value of HSAs in retirement planning extends well beyond immediate healthcare savings. Unlike Flexible Spending Accounts (FSAs), HSA funds roll over year to year and are portable between employers. After age 65, you can withdraw HSA funds for non-medical expenses without penalty (though you'll pay ordinary income tax), essentially functioning like a traditional IRA. However, the real power lies in preserving HSA funds for medical expenses, which remain tax-free regardless of when you incur them.

Healthcare expenses in retirement can be substantial, making HSA preservation strategies particularly valuable. A single 65-year-old retiring in 2025 could expect to spend $172,500 on medical expenses throughout retirement, according to Fidelity research. By maximizing HSA contributions during your working years and minimizing withdrawals, you can build a substantial tax-free fund specifically earmarked for these costs.

Investment options within HSAs further enhance their retirement value. Once your HSA balance reaches a minimum threshold (typically $1,000 to $2,000), most HSA providers allow you to invest funds in mutual funds, ETFs, or other investment vehicles. This investment growth occurs tax-free, and properly managed HSA investments can significantly outpace healthcare inflation over time.

For those approaching Medicare eligibility, timing becomes crucial. You must stop HSA contributions once you enroll in Medicare, even if you continue working and maintain HDHP coverage. However, you can continue using accumulated HSA funds tax-free for qualified medical expenses throughout retirement, including Medicare premiums, deductibles, and coinsurance.

Planning strategies for maximizing HSA value include contributing the maximum amount annually, investing HSA funds for long-term growth rather than using them for current medical expenses (if financially feasible), keeping detailed records of medical expenses that could be reimbursed from HSA funds years later, and coordinating HSA withdrawals with other retirement income to optimize your overall tax strategy.

Supplemental Insurance Options

While Medicare provides essential healthcare coverage, it leaves significant gaps that can result in substantial out-of-pocket costs. Supplemental insurance options help fill these gaps, with Medicare Supplement Insurance (Medigap) and Medicare Advantage being the two primary approaches.

Medigap policies are standardized by the federal government and sold by private insurance companies to work alongside Original Medicare. These policies help pay for costs that Medicare doesn't cover, such as coinsurance, copayments, and deductibles. For 2025, popular Medigap Plan G covers everything except the Medicare Part B deductible of $257, providing comprehensive protection against unexpected medical costs.

Medigap premiums vary significantly by insurance company, geographic location, and pricing method. Insurance companies use three primary pricing approaches: community-rated (same premium regardless of age), issue-age-rated (premium based on age when you buy), and attained-age-rated (premium increases as you age). Understanding these pricing differences can save thousands of dollars over time.

Plans K and L offer cost-sharing alternatives with lower monthly premiums but higher out-of-pocket costs. Plan K covers 50% of most benefits until you reach the annual out-of-pocket limit of $7,220 in 2025, after which it pays 100%. Plan L covers 75% of most benefits until you reach the $3,610 out-of-pocket limit.

Medicare Advantage (Part C) represents an alternative to Original Medicare plus Medigap, providing Part A and Part B benefits through private insurance plans. These plans often include prescription drug coverage and additional benefits like dental, vision, and hearing services. The average monthly premium for Medicare Advantage plans in 2025 is $17.00, down from $18.23 in 2024, though many plans charge no additional premium beyond Part B.

Medicare Advantage plans have out-of-pocket maximums, which Original Medicare lacks. For 2025, the maximum out-of-pocket limit is $9,350 for in-network services and $14,000 for combined in-network and out-of-network services. This protection provides crucial financial security against catastrophic medical costs.

When choosing between Medigap and Medicare Advantage, consider several factors. Medigap offers greater provider flexibility since it works with any doctor or hospital that accepts Medicare, while Medicare Advantage plans typically use provider networks. Medigap premiums are generally higher but provide more predictable costs, while Medicare Advantage plans often have lower premiums but variable copayments and coinsurance.

Long-term care insurance represents another crucial supplemental option, as neither Medicare nor Medigap covers extended nursing home stays or most home healthcare services. With the median annual cost of a private room in a nursing home exceeding $116,800, long-term care insurance can protect retirement savings from catastrophic care costs. Premiums for long-term care insurance for a healthy 60-year-old average $2,585 for males and $4,400 for females, but waiting until later ages significantly increases costs and reduces availability.

Dental, Vision, and Hearing Coverage

Original Medicare provides minimal coverage for dental, vision, and hearing services, creating significant gaps that can result in substantial out-of-pocket expenses. Understanding these limitations and available alternatives is crucial for comprehensive retirement healthcare planning.

Medicare's dental coverage is severely limited, covering only dental services that are "inextricably linked" to covered medical procedures. For example, Medicare might cover a dental exam before radiation treatment for head and neck cancer, or tooth extraction necessary before an organ transplant. Routine dental care, including cleanings, fillings, crowns, dentures, and periodontal treatment, receives no coverage under Original Medicare.

The financial impact of this coverage gap is substantial. According to KFF research, 53% of Medicare beneficiaries reported having a dental visit within the past year, with many facing significant out-of-pocket costs. Adults with diagnosed chronic conditions often have higher dental costs, as poor oral health correlates with increased risks of heart disease, diabetes, and other systemic conditions.

Vision coverage under Original Medicare is similarly limited, covering eye exams only when medically necessary to diagnose or treat diseases like glaucoma or diabetic retinopathy. Routine eye exams for prescription glasses or contact lenses receive no coverage, nor do prescription eyewear costs. Medicare will cover one pair of eyeglasses or contact lenses following cataract surgery with intraocular lens implantation, but this represents the extent of routine vision coverage.

Hearing services fare even worse under Original Medicare, which doesn't cover hearing aids or routine hearing exams for hearing aid fitting. Given that close to half (44%) of Medicare beneficiaries report difficulty hearing, this coverage gap affects millions of retirees. Hearing aids can cost thousands of dollars and typically need replacement every 3-5 years.

Medicare Advantage plans often include dental, vision, and hearing benefits, though coverage varies significantly by plan and provider. Many plans cover preventive dental care like cleanings and exams, with some offering allowances for more extensive treatments. Vision benefits typically include annual eye exams and allowances for prescription eyewear. Hearing benefits may include exams and discounts on hearing aids through preferred providers.

For those with Original Medicare, standalone insurance plans can help fill these gaps. Dental insurance plans typically cost $20-50 monthly and cover preventive care while providing allowances for major procedures. Vision insurance usually costs $15-25 monthly and includes eye exams plus allowances for glasses or contacts. However, these plans often have waiting periods, annual maximums, and limited networks.

Alternative approaches to managing these costs include discount plans, which negotiate reduced rates with participating providers in exchange for membership fees. Healthcare savings specifically earmarked for dental, vision, and hearing expenses can also help manage these predictable costs. Some employers offer retiree health benefits that include these services, making it worthwhile to investigate continued coverage options.

Community resources can provide additional support, particularly for hearing services. Local Lions Clubs often run programs distributing low-cost hearing aids to those in need, while organizations like Sertoma help connect people to state and national hearing assistance programs. The American Speech-Language-Hearing Association maintains directories of local agencies providing hearing services for those with limited resources.

Managing Chronic Conditions Cost-Effectively

Chronic conditions become increasingly common with age and represent one of the most significant drivers of healthcare costs in retirement. Adults who've been diagnosed with chronic conditions such as emphysema, diabetes, heart disease, and high blood pressure have much higher medical costs, with annual out-of-pocket costs increasing by 27% for diabetes, 55% for heart disease, and 19% for high blood pressure compared to those without these conditions.

Understanding the financial impact of chronic conditions is crucial for retirement planning. Ninety percent of the nation's $4.9 trillion in annual healthcare expenditures are for people with chronic and mental health conditions, highlighting the outsized impact these conditions have on healthcare costs. The economic burden extends beyond direct medical costs to include lost productivity, family caregiving time, and quality of life impacts.

Effective management of chronic conditions requires a proactive, multi-faceted approach that emphasizes prevention, early intervention, and cost-effective treatment strategies. Preventive care represents one of the most powerful tools for managing chronic condition costs, as early detection and treatment can prevent complications that result in expensive emergency interventions.

Medicare covers many preventive services at no cost, including annual wellness visits, screenings for diabetes, cardiovascular disease, and various cancers, and vaccinations. Taking advantage of these covered services can help detect chronic conditions early when they're more manageable and less expensive to treat. Additionally, lifestyle modifications such as regular exercise, healthy diet, and smoking cessation can significantly reduce both the risk of developing chronic conditions and the severity of existing conditions.

Medication management represents another critical component of cost-effective chronic condition management. The Medicare Part D coverage gap elimination in 2025 and the $2,000 annual out-of-pocket cap provide significant relief for those with high prescription drug costs. However, additional strategies can further reduce medication expenses, including using generic medications when available, exploring manufacturer patient assistance programs, comparing prices across different pharmacies, and working with healthcare providers to optimize medication regimens.

Care coordination becomes increasingly important for managing multiple chronic conditions, which affect a significant percentage of Medicare beneficiaries. Integrated care approaches that coordinate between primary care physicians, specialists, and other healthcare providers can reduce duplicate testing, prevent adverse drug interactions, and ensure that treatment plans are comprehensive and effective.

Technology tools are increasingly valuable for chronic condition management, including remote monitoring devices, medication management apps, and telehealth services. Medicare has expanded coverage for telehealth services, making it easier to access care without the time and cost of travel. These tools can help identify problems early, improve medication adherence, and reduce the need for expensive emergency interventions.

Financial strategies for managing chronic condition costs include maximizing the use of HSA funds for medical expenses, taking advantage of Medicare's chronic care management services (which are covered under Part B), exploring Medicare Special Needs Plans (SNPs) designed for specific chronic conditions, and investigating state and federal assistance programs that may help with medication costs or other expenses.

Planning for potential care needs as chronic conditions progress is essential. This includes understanding what services Medicare does and doesn't cover, exploring supplemental insurance options that provide additional coverage for services you're likely to need, and considering long-term care insurance to protect against the costs of extended care that chronic conditions might necessitate.

Family and caregiver support plays a crucial role in cost-effective chronic condition management. Family caregivers provide an estimated $234 billion worth of unpaid care annually, and supporting these caregivers through education, respite services, and other resources can help prevent caregiver burnout and the resulting increased formal care costs.

Conclusion

Managing healthcare costs in retirement requires a comprehensive, proactive approach that goes far beyond simply enrolling in Medicare. The $172,500 that a 65-year-old retiring in 2025 can expect to spend on healthcare throughout retirement represents a substantial portion of most retirees' budgets, making strategic planning essential for financial security.

Success in managing these costs requires understanding the true scope of Medicare coverage and its limitations, maximizing tax-advantaged savings vehicles like HSAs during your working years, carefully evaluating supplemental insurance options based on your individual needs and circumstances, planning for gaps in dental, vision, and hearing coverage that Medicare doesn't address, and developing cost-effective strategies for managing chronic conditions that become more common with age.

The key to long-term success lies in starting early and taking a holistic approach to healthcare cost planning. This means integrating healthcare cost projections into your overall retirement planning, staying informed about changes in Medicare and supplemental insurance options, maintaining your health through preventive care and healthy lifestyle choices, and building sufficient savings to handle both expected and unexpected healthcare expenses.

Remember that healthcare cost management in retirement is not a one-time decision but an ongoing process that requires regular review and adjustment as your health needs, financial situation, and available options evolve. By implementing the strategies outlined in this chapter and working with qualified professionals when needed, you can protect both your health and your financial security throughout your retirement years.

The investment in proper healthcare cost planning today will pay dividends in the form of reduced financial stress, better health outcomes, and preserved retirement savings throughout your golden years.

Healthcare costs may be inevitable in retirement, but with proper planning and management, they don't have to derail your retirement dreams or compromise your financial security.

CHAPTER 15: CREATING YOUR PERSONAL RETIREMENT HEALTHCARE STRATEGY

Creating a personal retirement healthcare strategy is perhaps the most crucial yet challenging aspect of retirement planning. With healthcare costs representing one of the largest and most unpredictable expenses in retirement, developing a comprehensive strategy tailored to your unique circumstances can mean the difference between financial security and financial distress in your golden years. This process requires careful assessment of your individual needs, strategic timing of Medicare and Social Security enrollment decisions, ongoing review and adjustment of your plans, and leveraging professional resources when appropriate.

The complexity of healthcare planning in retirement cannot be overstated. Recent research reveals that 55% of Americans anticipate it will be difficult to enroll in Medicare coverage, and half expect to be confused when selecting a plan. More concerning, one in five Americans report they have never considered healthcare needs during retirement—a figure that rises to one in four among Gen X. With the average 65-year-old retiring in 2025 expected to spend $172,500 on healthcare throughout retirement, the cost of inadequate planning can be devastating. This chapter will guide you through the systematic process of creating a personalized healthcare strategy that addresses your specific needs, timeline, and circumstances while positioning you for ongoing success throughout your retirement years.

Assessing Your Individual Needs

The foundation of any effective retirement healthcare strategy begins with a thorough assessment of your individual needs, circumstances, and risk factors. This comprehensive evaluation should encompass your current health status, family medical history, lifestyle factors, financial situation, and personal preferences regarding healthcare and retirement living arrangements.

Your current health status serves as the starting point for projecting future healthcare needs and costs. Begin by documenting your existing medical conditions, prescription medications, and ongoing treatments. Research shows that adults with chronic conditions face significantly higher medical costs, with annual out-of-pocket expenses increasing by 27% for diabetes, 55% for heart disease, and 19% for high blood pressure compared to those without these conditions. Understanding your current health trajectory allows for more accurate planning and budgeting.

Family medical history provides crucial insights into potential future health risks. Consider the longevity, chronic conditions, and causes of death among your parents, grandparents, and siblings. While genetics don't determine destiny, they offer valuable information for planning purposes. If your family history suggests increased risk for conditions like heart disease, diabetes, or Alzheimer's disease, factor these possibilities into your healthcare strategy and financial planning.

Lifestyle factors significantly influence both health outcomes and healthcare costs in retirement. Regular exercise, healthy diet, smoking cessation, and stress management can dramatically reduce the risk of chronic conditions and their associated costs. Conversely, sedentary lifestyle, poor nutrition, smoking, and excessive alcohol consumption increase both health risks and potential healthcare expenses. Honestly assess your current lifestyle and consider what changes you're willing and able to make to improve your health trajectory.

Geographic considerations play a substantial role in healthcare planning. Healthcare costs vary significantly by region, with some areas having costs 20-30% above the national average while others fall well below. Additionally, access to quality healthcare providers, proximity to family support systems, and availability of senior services differ markedly between locations. If you're considering relocating in retirement, research healthcare costs and quality in your target destination.

Financial resources available for healthcare represent another critical component of your needs assessment. Calculate your projected retirement income from all sources, including Social Security, pensions, retirement account withdrawals, and any continuing employment income. Determine what percentage of this income you can realistically allocate to healthcare expenses, keeping in mind that financial advisors typically recommend budgeting 15% of retirement income for healthcare costs.

Support systems and care preferences require careful consideration as part of your needs assessment. Evaluate your family situation, including the proximity and availability of adult children or other relatives who might provide assistance. Consider your preferences for aging in place versus moving to a retirement community or assisted living facility. These preferences significantly impact both costs and healthcare planning requirements.

Insurance history and coverage gaps should be thoroughly documented. Review your current health insurance, including any employer-sponsored retiree health benefits you may be eligible for. Understand the coverage provided, costs involved, and how these benefits coordinate with Medicare. Identify any gaps in coverage that will need to be addressed through Medicare supplements or other insurance products.

Risk tolerance for healthcare costs varies significantly among individuals and impacts strategy development. Some retirees prefer predictable costs through comprehensive insurance coverage, even if premiums are higher. Others are comfortable with higher deductibles and out-of-pocket exposure in exchange for lower premiums. Understanding your risk tolerance helps determine the appropriate balance between insurance coverage and self-insurance through savings.

Technology comfort and adoption affect healthcare access and costs in modern retirement. Telehealth services, remote monitoring devices, and digital health management tools are increasingly important for cost-effective care delivery. Assess your current comfort level with technology and willingness to adopt new tools that could improve your healthcare outcomes while reducing costs.

Building Your Medicare and Social Security Timeline

Creating a detailed timeline for Medicare enrollment and Social Security claiming decisions is essential for avoiding costly penalties and maximizing benefits. These decisions are interconnected and require careful coordination to optimize your overall retirement healthcare and income strategy.

Your Medicare Initial Enrollment Period begins three months before the month you turn 65 and extends through three months after your 65th birthday month, creating a seven-month window for enrollment. If you're already receiving Social Security benefits at least four months before turning 65, you'll be automatically enrolled in Medicare Parts A and B, with coverage beginning the month you turn 65 (or the month before if your birthday falls on the first of the month).

For those not automatically enrolled, active enrollment decisions are required. If you're still working and have employer-sponsored health insurance that provides creditable coverage, you may choose to delay Medicare Part B enrollment without penalty. However, this decision requires careful analysis of your employer coverage compared to Medicare benefits and costs. Your employer's human resources department should provide documentation of whether your coverage is considered creditable.

Social Security claiming decisions significantly impact your Medicare timeline and overall retirement strategy. You can begin claiming Social Security benefits as early as age 62, but doing so permanently reduces your monthly benefits. Waiting until your full retirement age (67 for those born in 1960 or later) provides full benefits, while delaying until age 70 maximizes your monthly payments. Research indicates that waiting until age 70 to claim Social Security can boost benefit checks by 24% compared to claiming at full retirement age.

The intersection of Medicare and Social Security decisions creates important coordination opportunities. If you delay Social Security benefits beyond age 65, you'll need to actively enroll in Medicare Part A and potentially Part B, depending on your employment status and insurance coverage. Medicare Part A is premium-free for most beneficiaries and generally should be claimed at age 65 even if you delay Social Security benefits.

Medicare Part B enrollment timing depends heavily on your employment and insurance status. If you have creditable employer coverage, you can delay Part B enrollment and use a Special Enrollment Period to enroll within eight months of losing employer coverage or stopping work, whichever comes first. However, if your employer coverage isn't creditable or you're not working, delaying Part B enrollment results in permanent penalties of 10% for each 12-month period you could have had Part B but didn't sign up.

Medicare Part C (Medicare Advantage) and Part D (prescription drug coverage) enrollment follows the same timeline as Original Medicare, with additional considerations. If you choose Medicare Advantage, you typically cannot also purchase Medigap coverage. Part D enrollment should generally occur during your Initial Enrollment Period unless you have creditable prescription drug coverage through an employer or other source.

Creating your personal timeline requires mapping out these decisions based on your specific circumstances. For someone planning to retire at 62 with no employer retiree health benefits, the timeline might include claiming Social Security at 62, securing individual health insurance through age 65, enrolling in Medicare at 65, and evaluating Medigap or Medicare Advantage options. Conversely, someone working until 67 with employer health insurance might delay Social Security until full retirement age, enroll in Medicare Part A at 65 while maintaining employer coverage, and transition to Medicare Part B upon retirement.

Special circumstances require modified timelines. If you have End-Stage Renal Disease (ESRD), you may be eligible for Medicare before age 65. Those receiving Social Security disability benefits become eligible for Medicare after 24 months of disability benefits. Individuals with ALS (Lou Gehrig's disease) qualify for Medicare immediately upon receiving disability benefits.

Consider the tax implications of your Medicare and Social Security timeline. Social Security benefits may be subject to federal income tax depending on your combined income, and Medicare premiums can be affected by your income through the Income-Related Monthly Adjustment Amount (IRMAA). Coordinating these decisions with your overall retirement income strategy can minimize tax impacts and reduce Medicare premium surcharges.

Documentation and deadline tracking are crucial components of your timeline. Create a calendar marking key dates such as your 65th birthday, Medicare enrollment deadlines, Social Security application timing, and any employer coverage termination dates. Gather necessary documents including birth certificates, marriage certificates (if applicable), tax returns, and employer coverage documentation well in advance of enrollment deadlines.

Annual Review and Adjustment Strategies

Retirement healthcare planning is not a one-time event but an ongoing process requiring regular review and adjustment as circumstances change. Medicare plans, health needs, financial situations, and available options evolve continuously, making annual reviews essential for maintaining an optimal healthcare strategy.

Medicare's Annual Open Enrollment Period, running from October 15 to December 7 each year, provides the primary opportunity to make changes to your Medicare coverage. During this period, you can switch between Original Medicare and Medicare Advantage, change Medicare Advantage plans, add or drop prescription drug coverage, or switch Part D plans. Any changes made during this period take effect January 1 of the following year.

Conducting a comprehensive annual review involves evaluating multiple aspects of your healthcare situation. Begin by assessing changes in your health status, including new diagnoses, medications, or treatment needs that might affect your insurance requirements. Review your current plan's provider network to ensure your doctors and hospitals remain covered, as networks can change annually.

Prescription drug coverage requires particular attention during annual reviews. Medicare Part D plans frequently change their formularies (lists of covered drugs), and your medications may move to different cost-sharing tiers or require prior authorization. Compare your current drug costs with alternative plans using Medicare's Plan Finder tool, which provides personalized cost estimates based on your specific medications.

Medicare Advantage plans can significantly alter their benefits, costs, and provider networks each year. Review your plan's Annual Notice of Change (ANOC) and Evidence of Coverage (EOC) documents, which detail any modifications for the upcoming year. Pay particular attention to changes in premiums, deductibles, copayments, provider networks, and additional benefits like dental, vision, or hearing coverage.

For those with Original Medicare and Medigap coverage, annual reviews should focus on whether your current supplemental insurance continues to meet your needs and remains competitively priced. While

Medigap benefits are standardized, premiums can vary significantly between insurance companies, and shopping for better rates can result in substantial savings.

Financial circumstances changes warrant strategy adjustments. Increases or decreases in income can affect Medicare premium costs through IRMAA adjustments, which are based on tax returns from two years prior. Changes in retirement account balances, investment performance, or other financial factors may necessitate modifications to your healthcare budget allocation or insurance coverage levels.

Geographic relocations, whether permanent moves or extended seasonal residences, require healthcare strategy updates. Medicare Advantage plans have specific service areas, and moving outside your plan's coverage area triggers a Special Enrollment Period allowing plan changes. Even within the same state, different regions may have varying plan options and provider networks.

Family situation changes can significantly impact healthcare planning. Marriage, divorce, or the death of a spouse affects Social Security benefits, Medicare enrollment options, and household healthcare budgeting. Adult children's proximity and availability for assistance may change, influencing decisions about aging in place versus alternative living arrangements.

Technology adoption presents ongoing opportunities for healthcare cost management and improved outcomes. Telehealth services, remote monitoring devices, and digital health management tools continue evolving rapidly. Regular assessment of these options can identify new opportunities for more convenient and cost-effective care delivery.

Medicare plan quality ratings, published annually by CMS, provide valuable information for plan comparison. Five-star rating systems evaluate plan performance across multiple domains including health outcomes, member experience, and care coordination. Plans with higher ratings often provide better value and outcomes for beneficiaries.

Documentation and record-keeping support effective annual reviews. Maintain files containing your current insurance documents, provider contact information, medication lists, and healthcare expense records. Track your annual out-of-pocket spending to understand patterns and identify opportunities for cost reduction.

Timing considerations affect review effectiveness. Begin your annual review process in early fall, well before the October 15 enrollment deadline. This allows sufficient time for thorough research, consultations with healthcare providers or advisors, and careful decision-making without deadline pressure.

Working with Professionals: When and How

Navigating the complexities of retirement healthcare planning often requires professional assistance. Understanding when to seek help, what types of professionals are available, and how to work effectively with them can significantly improve your planning outcomes while avoiding costly mistakes.

State Health Insurance Assistance Programs (SHIPs) represent the most accessible and cost-effective professional resource for Medicare-related guidance. These federally funded programs provide free, unbiased counseling and assistance to Medicare beneficiaries and their families. With 54 SHIP programs operating in all 50 states, Puerto Rico, Guam, the District of Columbia, and the U.S. Virgin Islands, SHIPs maintain a network of more than 12,500 trained volunteers and staff members.

SHIP counselors provide one-on-one assistance with Medicare enrollment decisions, plan comparisons, appeals processes, and benefits coordination. They can help you understand the differences between Original Medicare and Medicare Advantage, evaluate Medigap options, compare prescription drug plans, and identify potential cost-saving programs. SHIP services are particularly valuable during Initial Enrollment Periods and Annual Open Enrollment Periods when decision complexity is highest.

Licensed insurance agents specializing in Medicare products offer another professional resource, though their services differ fundamentally from SHIP counselors. Insurance agents are compensated through commissions from insurance companies and can enroll you in Medicare Advantage, Medigap, and Part D plans. While agents can provide valuable market knowledge and enrollment assistance, remember that their recommendations may be influenced by compensation structures.

Financial advisors with expertise in retirement and healthcare planning can provide comprehensive guidance integrating Medicare decisions with broader financial strategies. Fee-only financial advisors, who are compensated directly by clients rather than through product sales, can offer unbiased advice on healthcare cost budgeting, HSA strategies, and insurance decision-making. Look for advisors with credentials such as CFP (Certified Financial Planner) and specific experience in retirement healthcare planning.

Elder law attorneys specialize in legal issues affecting seniors, including Medicare appeals, Medicaid planning, and estate planning coordination with healthcare needs. Their services become particularly valuable when dealing with complex family situations, long-term care planning, or disputes with insurance providers. Elder law attorneys can also assist with advance directives, power of attorney documents, and other legal preparations for aging.

Healthcare advocates and geriatric care managers provide professional assistance with healthcare navigation and coordination. These professionals can help manage complex medical situations, coordinate care between multiple providers, and advocate for appropriate services and coverage. Their services are particularly valuable for individuals with multiple chronic conditions or complex care needs.

Knowing when to seek professional assistance can save both money and stress. Consider professional help when facing initial Medicare enrollment decisions, especially if you have complex health conditions or employer retiree benefits. Annual plan reviews benefit from professional assistance if your circumstances have changed significantly or if you're overwhelmed by the number of available options. Appeals processes for denied claims or coverage decisions often require professional advocacy to navigate successfully.

Preparing for professional consultations maximizes their value and efficiency. Gather relevant documents including current insurance cards, medication lists, provider information, tax returns (for income verification), and any employer benefits documentation. Prepare specific questions about your situation and priorities. Be honest about your health status, financial circumstances, and preferences, as this information is crucial for receiving appropriate guidance.

Evaluating professional qualifications ensures you're working with competent, trustworthy advisors. Verify credentials through appropriate professional organizations and state licensing boards. For insurance agents, check state insurance department websites for licensing verification and any complaint history. For financial advisors, use FINRA's BrokerCheck database and the SEC's Investment Adviser Public Disclosure website.

Understanding professional limitations and potential conflicts of interest helps set appropriate expectations. SHIP counselors cannot recommend specific insurance companies or products but provide education and comparison tools. Insurance agents may have limited product offerings based on their company appointments. Financial advisors may have minimum account sizes or fee structures that affect accessibility.

Cost considerations vary significantly among professional services. SHIP services are completely free, funded by federal and state grants. Insurance agent services are typically provided at no direct cost, with compensation coming from insurance company commissions. Financial advisor fees range from hourly consultations to ongoing asset-based management fees. Elder law attorney fees are typically hourly or project-based.

Building ongoing relationships with appropriate professionals can provide long-term value as your needs evolve. Consider establishing relationships with a trusted SHIP counselor, qualified insurance agent, and financial advisor who understands your situation. These relationships can provide continuity and personalized service as you navigate changing healthcare needs and options throughout retirement.

Resources and Tools for Ongoing Education

Staying informed about Medicare changes, healthcare costs, and planning strategies requires accessing reliable, up-to-date information sources. The complexity and frequent changes in healthcare policy and insurance options make ongoing education essential for maintaining an effective retirement healthcare strategy.

Medicare.gov serves as the official government source for Medicare information and provides numerous tools for beneficiaries. The Medicare Plan Finder allows you to compare costs and coverage for Medicare Advantage, Medigap, and Part D plans based on your specific location, medications, and preferred providers. The site's "What's Medicare" section provides comprehensive educational materials about all aspects of Medicare coverage, enrollment, and rights.

The Social Security Administration website (ssa.gov) offers essential information about Medicare enrollment coordination with Social Security benefits. Their Medicare section explains automatic enrollment processes, timing considerations, and the relationship between Social Security and Medicare decisions. The site also provides access to your personal Social Security statement and benefit estimation tools.

Medicare Rights Center (medicarerights.org) provides independent consumer advocacy and education resources. Their publications include detailed guides on Medicare topics, rights and protections, and assistance programs. They also operate a helpline providing personalized assistance with Medicare questions and problems.

AARP Medicare information resources offer extensive educational materials targeted specifically to seniors. Their Medicare section includes plan comparison tools, cost calculators, and articles on current Medicare issues. AARP's annual Medicare guide provides comprehensive information about coverage options and changes for the upcoming year.

Kaiser Family Foundation (kff.org) produces research and analysis on Medicare policy, costs, and trends. Their Medicare section provides data and reports that help understand the broader context of Medicare issues and policy developments. This information is particularly valuable for understanding how policy changes might affect your coverage and costs.

Professional organization websites provide specialized information for specific aspects of healthcare planning. The National Association of Insurance Commissioners (naic.org) offers consumer guides on Medigap insurance and long-term care planning. The Financial Planning Association (onefpa.org) provides resources for finding qualified financial advisors and educational materials on retirement planning.

Technology tools and mobile applications enhance access to healthcare information and management. Medicare's official mobile app provides plan comparison tools and account management features. Prescription drug cost comparison apps help identify the most cost-effective pharmacy options. Personal health record apps assist with organizing medical information and tracking healthcare expenses.

News sources specializing in senior issues and healthcare policy provide timely updates on changes affecting Medicare and retirement healthcare planning. Publications such as Next Avenue, Senior Planet, and Aging Today offer articles on current issues, policy changes, and practical guidance for navigating healthcare in retirement.

Educational webinars and seminars offer structured learning opportunities on healthcare planning topics. Many organizations, including SHIP programs, libraries, senior centers, and financial services firms, offer free educational programs. These sessions often include question-and-answer opportunities and current information about plan changes and enrollment periods.

Government publication resources provide authoritative information on various aspects of retirement healthcare planning. The Department of Health and Human Services publishes annual Medicare handbooks and guides. The Internal Revenue Service provides information about HSAs and tax implications of healthcare expenses. The Department of Labor offers retirement planning resources that include healthcare cost considerations.

Creating a personalized information strategy helps manage the volume of available resources and ensures you stay current on relevant topics. Identify 3-4 primary sources that you'll check regularly for updates. Subscribe to email newsletters from trusted sources to receive important updates. Set calendar reminders for key dates such as Annual Open Enrollment Periods and plan review deadlines.

Verifying information accuracy is crucial when using multiple sources. Cross-reference important information with official government sources before making decisions. Be wary of sources with obvious commercial interests or those promoting specific products. When in doubt, consult with SHIP counselors or other qualified professionals to verify information.

Staying organized with collected information enhances its usefulness for decision-making. Create digital or physical files for Medicare information, Social Security documents, insurance plan materials, and educational resources. Maintain a healthcare planning checklist that includes key dates, deadlines, and action items. Review and update your information files annually during your healthcare plan review process.

Conclusion

Creating your personal retirement healthcare strategy is a comprehensive process that requires careful assessment, strategic planning, and ongoing attention throughout your retirement years. The complexity of Medicare, the variability of healthcare costs, and the personal nature of health and financial circumstances make this planning both challenging and essential.

Success in retirement healthcare planning comes from taking a systematic approach that begins with honest assessment of your individual needs, circumstances, and preferences. Understanding your health status, family history, financial resources, and risk tolerance provides the foundation for making informed decisions about insurance coverage, care preferences, and budget allocation.

Building an effective Medicare and Social Security timeline ensures you maximize benefits while avoiding costly penalties. The interconnected nature of these decisions requires careful coordination and advance planning to optimize your overall retirement income and healthcare coverage strategy.

Regular review and adjustment of your healthcare strategy keeps pace with changing circumstances, evolving needs, and new opportunities. The dynamic nature of Medicare plans, prescription drug formularies, and healthcare options makes annual reviews essential for maintaining optimal coverage and costs.

Professional resources provide valuable assistance throughout your healthcare planning journey. From free SHIP counseling to specialized advisory services, knowing when and how to access professional help can significantly improve your planning outcomes while reducing stress and avoiding mistakes.

Ongoing education through reliable resources and tools keeps you informed and empowered to make sound decisions as your needs and circumstances evolve. The investment in staying current on Medicare changes, healthcare policy developments, and planning strategies pays dividends in better outcomes and reduced costs.

Remember that healthcare planning in retirement is not about achieving perfection but about making informed decisions that align with your values, circumstances, and goals. The key is to start early, stay informed, review regularly, and adjust as needed. With thoughtful planning and ongoing attention, you can create a healthcare strategy that provides security, peace of mind, and the foundation for a healthy, financially secure retirement.

CHAPTER 16: COMMON MISTAKES AND HOW TO AVOID THEM

Making the right decisions about Medicare and Social Security can feel overwhelming, especially when the consequences of getting it wrong can last a lifetime. The reality is stark: Medicare late enrollment penalties are permanent charges that stay with you for as long as you have coverage, and Social Security claiming mistakes can cost tens of thousands of dollars over your retirement. These aren't just temporary setbacks—they're financial decisions that compound over decades.

The good news is that most of these costly errors are entirely preventable with the right knowledge and planning. Research shows that about 20% of people paying Medicare Part B late enrollment penalties didn't even know about these penalties when they first became eligible at age 65. This chapter will walk you through the most common mistakes people make with Medicare and Social Security, helping you avoid the pitfalls that catch so many retirees off guard. Understanding these mistakes isn't just about protecting your wallet—it's about securing your peace of mind and ensuring your retirement years are as financially stable as possible.

The Top 10 Medicare Mistakes

1. Missing Your Initial Enrollment Period

Your Initial Enrollment Period begins three months before you turn 65, includes the month you turn 65, and extends three months after. Missing this seven-month window is one of the costliest mistakes you can make. For Medicare Part B, you'll pay a 10% penalty for each 12-month period you could have signed up but didn't. If you delay five years, that's a permanent 50% increase to your monthly premium.

Example: If the standard Part B premium is $185 in 2025 and you waited two full years to enroll, you'll pay $222 monthly ($185 plus a 20% penalty of $37) for as long as you have Medicare.

The only exception is if you have creditable coverage through active employment. If you're a federal employee working past 65, you can delay Medicare enrollment without penalty thanks to the Special Enrollment Period, which lasts eight months after you retire.

2. Not Understanding Creditable Coverage

Creditable prescription drug coverage is coverage that meets Medicare's minimum standards and is expected to pay, on average, at least as much as Medicare's standard prescription drug coverage. This includes some employer-based coverage, TRICARE, VA benefits, and qualified State Pharmaceutical Assistance Programs.

The mistake many people make is assuming all employer coverage is creditable. Always ask your HR department for a creditable coverage letter before declining Part D. If you go 63 days or more without creditable drug coverage, you'll face a Part D penalty of 1% of the national base beneficiary premium ($36.78 in 2025) for each month you delayed.

3. Automatic Enrollment Assumptions

You won't be automatically enrolled in Medicare at age 65 unless you receive Social Security benefits at least four months before your 65th birthday. Many people working past 65 assume they'll be notified when to enroll—they won't. You must take action during your Initial Enrollment Period.

4. Choosing Plans Based on Extras Alone

Don't pick a Medicare Advantage plan based only on extras offered beyond Original Medicare. Medicare Advantage plans typically have provider networks, and the rules depend on the type of plan. That dental benefit won't help if your doctors aren't in the network.

Always verify that your healthcare providers accept the plan before enrolling. Contact your doctors or other service providers to determine whether they're in your plan's network.

5. Ignoring Out-of-Pocket Limits

In 2025, Medicare Advantage plans have maximum out-of-pocket limits of $9,350 for covered in-network services and $14,000 for covered in-network and out-of-network services combined. Some plans have lower limits, but you need to understand what you might owe in a worst-case scenario.

For Medicare Supplement (Medigap) insurance, you aren't allowed to buy a Medigap plan if you're enrolled in a Medicare Advantage plan. Timing matters—you have a six-month Open Enrollment period when you first get Part B to buy Medigap without health underwriting.

6. Part D Coverage Gaps

All Part D plans have a $2,000 out-of-pocket limit in 2025, but understanding the coverage stages is crucial. After you reach your deductible (maximum $590 in 2025), you'll pay 25% coinsurance for generic and brand-name drugs until your out-of-pocket spending reaches $2,000.

Even if you don't take many medications now, consider getting a low-premium drug plan to avoid future penalties. The Part D late enrollment penalty is added to your premium for as long as you have Medicare drug coverage, even if you switch plans.

7. COBRA Coordination Confusion

Medicare coordinates differently with COBRA than it does with active coverage. When you're on COBRA, Medicare becomes primary, making COBRA secondary. This often makes COBRA coverage expensive and less valuable compared to Medicare with a supplement plan.

8. HSA Account Complications

If your health insurance plan is HSA-compatible and you wish to continue contributing to that account, you cannot be enrolled in any part of Medicare. Enrolling in any part of Medicare, including Part A, makes you ineligible to contribute to a Health Savings Account.

9. Employer Size Confusion

If you have group health plan coverage through an employer with 20 or more employees, the group plan pays first and Medicare pays second. If your employer has fewer than 20 employees, Medicare pays first and the group plan pays second. This affects whether you can safely delay Part B enrollment.

10. Income-Related Monthly Adjustment Amounts (IRMAA)

High-income beneficiaries pay additional amounts for Parts B and D based on their modified adjusted gross income from two years prior. These IRMAA surcharges can significantly increase your Medicare costs. Plan for potential increases if you have substantial retirement account withdrawals, pension payments, or investment income.

Social Security Claiming Errors That Cost You Money

Claiming Social Security at age 62 instead of waiting until full retirement age can reduce your benefits by up to 30%, depending on your birth year. For every year you wait between 62 and 70, you get a bump in benefits of about 5% to 8%—a guaranteed return that's tough to replicate elsewhere.

Real Impact: Lifetime benefits for a 65-year-old couple with one average and one low wage earner typically total about $1.1 million—but depending on timing, they could be hundreds of thousands more, or less.

Not Understanding Full Retirement Age

Full retirement age is 67 for anyone born in 1960 or later. Many people mistakenly think it's still 65. If you aren't aware of this change and plan on claiming benefits at age 66 years and 8 months in 2025, you'll technically be filing early, locking in a 1.11% reduction forever.

Earnings Limit Violations

In 2025, if you claim Social Security before your full retirement age and continue working, your benefits may be reduced if your earnings exceed $22,320 annually. For every $2 earned over the limit, $1 is deducted from your benefits.

In the year you reach full retirement age, the limit increases to $62,160, with $1 deducted for every $3 earned over this limit. While withheld amounts are eventually credited back, the short-term cash flow impact can be devastating.

Spousal Benefit Oversights

Spousal benefits are one of the most misunderstood aspects of Social Security. If you're married, divorced, or widowed, you may be eligible to receive benefits based on your spouse's (or former spouse's) work record—even if you never worked yourself.

When there are two earners, it might be better for one (typically the higher earner) to delay while the lower earner claims early. That way you're bringing in some Social Security income if you need it, while the higher-earning spouse waits until age 70 to get the biggest possible benefit.

Tax Planning Failures

Up to 85% of Social Security benefits may be taxable if combined income exceeds certain thresholds—$25,000 for individuals or $32,000 for joint filers. Many retirees fail to plan for this, leading to unexpected tax bills.

Fear-Based Claiming

Claiming benefits early because you think Social Security is going broke is frankly a pretty bad reason not to wait until your full retirement age. The latest Congressional Budget Office report says the Social Security trust fund will start to run short in 2033, but this doesn't mean no benefits will be paid. The country would still be able to pay about 80% of its Social Security obligations.

Not Coordinating as a Couple

No matter the circumstances, it's important to talk to your spouse before you sign up for benefits. If your spouse is entitled to Social Security too, you should coordinate a filing strategy together. Failing to coordinate can cost tens of thousands in lifetime benefits.

Earnings Record Errors

The SSA bases benefits on the highest 35 years of earnings, so errors in reported wages—often from past employers—result in lower calculations. You can check your earnings record online at any time if you have a My Social Security account. Millions overlook free annual statements from the SSA to correct discrepancies before claiming.

Not Reporting Life Changes

If a recipient marries, divorces, or experiences a shift in income, not notifying the Social Security Administration can result in overpayments that must be repaid, potentially halting future benefits until resolved. Each year, about two million people are told they owe the Social Security Administration money because the agency miscalculated their benefits and paid them too much.

Coordination Mistakes Between Medicare and Other Coverage

Who Pays First Confusion

The "primary payer" pays up to the limits of its coverage, then sends the rest of the balance to the "secondary payer." If the "secondary payer" doesn't cover the remaining balance, you may be responsible for the rest of costs.

Understanding coordination rules is crucial:

- If you have group health plan coverage through an employer with 20 or more employees, the group plan pays first and Medicare pays second
- If your employer has fewer than 20 employees, Medicare pays first and the group plan pays second
- If you have health insurance through a tribal health plan, Medicare pays first and the tribal health plan pays second

Not Notifying Providers of Coverage Changes

Tell your doctor and other health care providers about any changes in your insurance or coverage when you get care. Failing to inform providers about your coverage can result in incorrect billing and delayed payments.

TRICARE Coordination Issues

If you join a Medicare drug plan, TRICARE and your plan may coordinate their benefits if your plan's network pharmacy is also a TRICARE network pharmacy. Generally, if you are eligible for TRICARE For Life, TRICARE becomes the primary payer, and Medicare serves as the secondary payer.

VA Benefits Coordination

Generally, Medicare and the U.S. Department of Veterans Affairs (VA) can't pay for the same items or services. Each time you get health care or visit a provider, you'll have to choose which benefit to use.

Workers' Compensation Complications

If your provider knows you have a no-fault or liability insurance claim, they must try to get paid by the insurance company before billing Medicare. You're responsible for cooperating with the Benefits

Coordination & Recovery Center, Medicare Advantage, or Medicare drug plan's efforts to verify if claims are related to your workers' compensation settlement.

Conditional Payment Recovery

If the insurance company doesn't pay the claim promptly (usually within 120 days), your doctor or other provider may bill Medicare. Medicare may make a conditional payment to pay the bill, and then later recover any payments the primary payer should've made.

Documentation and Record-Keeping Best Practices

Essential Medicare Documents to Keep

Maintaining proper documentation is critical for avoiding problems and appeals. Keep these documents organized and easily accessible:

Enrollment Documents:

- Medicare cards (keep old ones until you receive new ones)
- Enrollment confirmations for Parts A, B, C, and D
- Special Enrollment Period documentation
- Creditable coverage letters from employers

Financial Records:

- Premium payment records
- Explanation of Benefits (EOB) statements
- Annual Medicare Summary Notices
- Tax documents related to Medicare premiums and IRMAA

Medical Records:

- Treatment records supporting medical necessity
- Prescription medication lists and histories
- Prior authorization approvals
- Appeal documentation and decisions

Social Security Documentation Requirements

Essential Documents:

- Social Security Administration correspondence
- Annual Social Security statements
- Benefit verification letters
- Tax documents (1099-SSA forms)

Life Event Documentation:

- Marriage certificates
- Divorce decrees
- Death certificates
- Employment verification letters

Record Retention Guidelines

HIPAA requires covered entities to retain documentation for at least 6 years after it was last in force. The Centers for Medicare & Medicaid Services requires records of healthcare providers submitting cost reports to be retained for at least five years after closure of the cost report.

Best Practices:

- Store records in a secure location, such as a locked cabinet or a HIPAA-compliant cloud storage service
- Use HIPAA-compliant methods to share documents, such as secure email or a secure file-sharing service
- Implement access controls to ensure that only authorized individuals can access patient records
- Create digital copies of physical documents
- Organize documents by year and type
- Review and update files annually

Documentation for Appeals

If you believe you were either overpaid or underpaid by Social Security, tell the SSA as soon as possible. Failing to report the error in a timely way can lead to months of incorrect payments along with the eventual hassle of sorting it out.

Keep detailed records of:

- All correspondence with Medicare and Social Security
- Phone call logs (date, time, representative name, reference number)
- Medical records supporting your case
- Financial documentation of out-of-pocket expenses
- Timeline of events leading to the issue

When to Seek Professional Help

Medicare Decision Points Requiring Expert Guidance

Complex Health Conditions: If you have multiple chronic conditions, take numerous medications, or require specialty care, a Medicare expert can help you navigate plan options that best meet your specific needs.

High-Income Situations: IRMAA surcharges can significantly impact your Medicare costs. If your income varies significantly or you have complex retirement account withdrawal strategies, professional guidance can help minimize these additional costs.

Employment Transitions: Coordinating Medicare with employer coverage requires understanding complex rules about creditable coverage, Special Enrollment Periods, and coordination of benefits. A professional can help ensure you don't face penalties while optimizing your coverage.

Multiple Coverage Sources: If you have VA benefits, TRICARE, employer coverage, or other insurance in addition to Medicare, professional help can ensure proper coordination and prevent billing issues.

Social Security Optimization Scenarios

Married Couples: Figuring out the precise claiming strategy for couples is complicated. Professional guidance can help you maximize lifetime benefits through strategic timing of claims.

Divorce Situations: Understanding spousal and survivor benefits based on ex-spouse's records requires expertise in complex Social Security rules.

Disability Transitions: Moving from Social Security Disability Insurance to retirement benefits involves timing considerations that affect your lifetime income.

High Earners: Complex strategies involving work continuation, taxation, and benefit optimization require professional analysis.

Types of Professional Help Available

State Health Insurance Assistance Programs (SHIP): Each state offers a SHIP, partly funded by the federal government, to give you free counseling and assistance. A SHIP counselor may be available by phone or in person.

Licensed Insurance Agents: Specialists in Medicare plans who can help you compare options and enroll in coverage. Ensure they're licensed in your state and certified to sell Medicare products.

Fee-Only Financial Planners: Can provide unbiased advice on Social Security optimization and Medicare planning as part of comprehensive retirement planning.

Elder Law Attorneys: Helpful for complex situations involving Medicaid planning, estate planning, or legal issues related to benefits.

Red Flags: When You Definitely Need Help

- You're facing Medicare or Social Security penalties
- You're being asked to repay benefits due to overpayments
- Your employer coverage is ending and you're unsure about timing
- You're considering working past age 65
- You have multiple health insurance options and complex medical needs
- You're dealing with denied claims or appeals
- You're facing IRMAA charges you believe are incorrect

Questions to Ask Professional Advisors

Before working with any professional, ask:

- What are your qualifications and certifications?
- How are you compensated? (fee-only, commission, hybrid)
- Do you have experience with situations like mine?
- Can you provide references from clients with similar needs?
- What specific services do you provide?
- How do you stay current on Medicare and Social Security rule changes?

Cost Considerations

- SHIP counseling is free
- Insurance agents are typically paid by insurance companies
- Financial planners may charge hourly rates or flat fees
- Be wary of anyone demanding upfront payments for Social Security optimization
- Get fee structures in writing before engaging services

The key to avoiding costly Medicare and Social Security mistakes is understanding your options, knowing the deadlines, and seeking help when situations become complex. The penalties for getting it wrong are severe and permanent, but with proper planning and professional guidance when needed, you can navigate these critical decisions successfully. Remember, the cost of professional advice is typically far less than the cost of making these mistakes on your own.

CONCLUSION

The Medicare and Social Security decisions you make in your 60s will impact your finances for the rest of your life. Late enrollment penalties become permanent fixtures in your monthly budget, and Social Security claiming mistakes can cost you hundreds of thousands of dollars over your retirement. But here's the encouraging truth: nearly every mistake outlined in this chapter is completely preventable with proper planning and knowledge.

Start preparing at least a year before you turn 65. Create a timeline of your enrollment periods, gather documentation of your current coverage, and understand your employer's benefits coordination rules. Keep meticulous records of all Medicare and Social Security correspondence, and don't hesitate to seek professional help when dealing with complex situations involving multiple coverage sources or optimization strategies.

Your future self will thank you for taking the time to get these critical decisions right. The peace of mind that comes from knowing you've maximized your benefits and avoided costly penalties is worth every hour you invest in proper planning today.

9 781257 865901